WHAT OTHER! SAYING...

If you are a link builder, content marketer or SEO, this book is required reading. Sage's book explains not just the "how's" but the "why's" as well so you understand the bigger picture. The advice given in this book is the real key to rankings in the search engines, and it's just not links, it's community participation (which this book explains). Well Done Sage, I'll be recommending that all our link builders at Internet Marketing Ninjas buy and read your book.

Jim Boykin Founder and CEO of Internet Marketing Ninjas. Owner of leading Internet marketing community Threadwatch, the Cre8aSiteForums, the Developer Shed properties, and Webmaster World.

Good stuff!

This book clearly guides readers around the rocky shores and hopefully will prevent shipwrecks. I particularly like that it is really preaching akin to our methodology: get links the old fashioned way... earn them! The last 2 paragraphs in the book said it all nicely.

The best tip is that any link that is easy to get is worthless, and may actually hurt you.

Bruce Clay President at Bruce Clay, Inc. and long-term icon in the search engine optimization community.

Sage Lewis has crafted an exceptional book on link building. He packs in a ton of tips and innovative techniques. His unmistakable personality shines through amid the invaluable advice that he presents with doses of his refreshing humor. Agencies and companies large and small will easily absorb link development options that they can put into place right away to achieve online marketing success.

A pioneer in the field of SEO, Mike Murray has been an executive at several agencies, including World Synergy and Fathom. Mike has shaped online marketing strategies for Little Tikes, Eaton Corp, Cleveland Clinic, FedEx Custom Critical, BISSELL, Woolite Carpet, Sauder, MTD, Career Education Corp. and many other businesses and organizations.

Mike Murray is the founder of onlinemarketingcoach.com where he and his team have helped small businesses grow online since 1997.

"*As the editor of this book, I have had the 'pleasure' of reading it 4 or more times. As a budding fiction author I find myself learning something new each time I read it that I'll be applying to my own link building strategies.*"
- Melissa "Rocky" Lewis, Writer

"*If you want to understand how to attract more people to your website on a consistent basis, read this book.*"
- Joe Pulizzi, CEO & Founder at Content Marketing Institute

I absolutely HATE link building. Which is why I've always hired people like Sage to do it for me. But Sage messed up. He took his deep, dark link building secrets and put them in his new book Link Building Is Dead by mistake. I've read it and you should too.

Jim Kukral is a 16-year Internet marketing professional who was recently named by Dun & Bradstreet as one of "The Most Influential Small Business People on Twitter."

Jim also serves as a Program Faculty Member for the University of San Francisco's Internet Marketing Program where he teaches classes to students around the globe on the topics of Internet marketing, entrepreneurship and social media.

<!--

I just want to say, "Wow" and "Thank you!"

These people are my heroes. Their kind words are humbling and deeply honoring. Their appreciation of this book make me want to work even harder at being a good contributor to an industry I deeply love.

- Sage

-->

LINK BUILDING IS DEAD

LONG LIVE
LINK BUILDING!

Link Building is Dead Long Live Link Building

Sage Lewis

If you find this book worthwhile, a link to it would be incredibly kind and greatly appreciated.
Just link here:
http://www.sagerock.com/linkbook

And so I can keep track of any discussion that may happen on Twitter, Facebook, Tumblr and Instagram please use this hashtag:
#sagelinks

"Always ask for the link."

Colophon

This book was written primarily on a VMWare Fusion
Windows 7 instance running on a Mac OS X Version 10.8.3
using Word 2007.

The book originated from over 70 articles published at
SearchEngineWatch.com by Sage Lewis. Although,
virtually all of articles have been updated to represent the
nature of link building in June 2013. The book also
includes a significant amount of original content.

The primary font of the book is Book Antiqua 12 point
using a CreateSpace Template of 5x8 inches. The book
cover font is League Gothic and the back cover font is
Century Gothic. The cover image is a photo taken by Sage
Lewis at the Great Lakes Medieval Faire and won
Honorable Mention in their photo contest.

The primary book editor is Melissa "Rocky" Lewis.

The cover design is by Sage Lewis.

The crazy action shot of Sage is by Tim Ash.

The book is self-published using CreateSpace.

This work is licensed under a Creative Commons
Attribution 3.0 Unported License.
(You can copy it. Just please reference it.)

ISBN: 978-0615829630

This book is dedicated to my wife, Rocky, who showed me that writing a book is possible.

Acknowledgements

Being that this is my first book, the acknowledgments section really could go on forever.

From my first grade teacher, Mrs. Clark, who took my mom and me to a Lynn Harrell cello concert and showed me anything is possible. To all the clients that have paid me enough to make a great salary and hire a few great people.

While there could be pages of this, I'll randomly pick a few people.

Greg Boser is key to all this. He hired me years ago as a contractor. He taught me a ton and paid me enough so I could quit my day job.

I also credit WebMasterWorld.com and its owner Brett Tabke for being the center for all my fundamental SEO learning early on.

My life would not be possible without 2 people: My wife, Rocky and my COO, Greg Habermann. Without them I would be floating in outer space.

Contents

Introduction

American Airlines still gives you the whole can of soda. I fly so much on low price carriers that I didn't know you could actually get 12 full ounces of beverage.

I struggled to drink it all as I poured Diet Coke again and again into my little plastic airplane cup – amazed I didn't have to make 4 ounces of beverage + ice last for the whole ride.

I drink soda all the time, but *that* Coke can felt special and that got me thinking about links. No really.

That day I got my glorious 12 ounces, I was flying to Kilgore Texas to talk to a group of community leaders about social media.

A lady in the back of the group asked, "How can I get more people to open my email newsletter?"

She sent emails to existing customers, once a quarter with a 10% open rate. That's low. When I asked about subject lines, she said it was always: "What's New at Company XYZ."

I asked, "What *is* new at your company?"

She got quiet. "Yeah...That's a good question."

Who is going to open an email when they know full well there's going to be nothing interesting in it? How the hell is someone going to find your company interesting when you don't even find your own company interesting?

We build links the exact same way. We ask people to link to us. Yet we offer them nothing interesting to reference. Products and services are not interesting. Sorry. You've got to dig deeper. You've got to find the real news, the love, the inspiration within your company. When you find (and upload) what is truly great about your firm, then you can ask people for links.

I hear people make excuses all the time. "But we are . . . a roofer, accountant, widget manufacturer, Boring Inc., an over-priced airline."

Listen. Inspiration doesn't have to be hard. Sometimes it can just be a full can of soda.

I didn't buy the ticket for the soda. I bought the ticket to get to Texas on time. But I tweeted, with a picture, about the soda. FlyerTalk forum is abuzz with soda stories. CNN wrote an article about an airline charging $1.99 for a full can.

There is a "soda" at your company. There is probably a whole case. Go find the news, find the thing that makes you different, better, inspiring. Only then can you expect links.

The Basics of Linking

What is a Link, why do sites need them, and how do I get them? We might as well start at the beginning. If you understand, I mean truly understand, what we are talking about here then you are going to have an easier time moving forward. These questions are answered in the following chapter.

What is a Link?

"Links" are connections from other Web sites pointing to your site with a hypertext link. Generally, when people discuss linking, they mean establishing inbound -- and only inbound -- connections from Web sites. Links that are evenly exchanged between sites, or reciprocal links, hold little value today. Outbound links -- going from your site to other sites -- offer few benefits from a search marketing perspective as well.

Why Do You Need Them?

All search engines value links as a measure of how influential and important a Web site is online. According to search engines, sites with many important, related sites linking to them must be worthwhile, therefore deserving a better ranking in the search listings.

What is PageRank?

Google created something called PageRank. It has gotten a great deal of press over the years. People have sued Google over PageRank. Today the value of PageRank is questionable. You can oftentimes see sites with lower PageRank outranking sites with higher PageRank. Just the same, it is useful to understand in this conversation because it has been so focused on for many years.

Sites are ranked on a scale of 1-10 in bell-shaped curve fashion. The number is best analyzed in relation to other sites in your industry because a 4 in some industries would be a top rank, but in another industry, it might take a 6 to indicate excellence in link building.

Link Popularity

Link popularity is probably a better, more meaningful phrase than PageRank.

Link popularity refers to how popular you are on the Web. Just remember all the painful experiences of high school and you will understand link popularity. If the head cheerleader or quarterback dates you, then you are popular. If The New York Times links to you, then you are popular. We'll talk more about all this. But I just wanted to set the stage.

There are then a whole other series of criteria like authority and proprietary rankings like MozRank. If you are looking for highly technical link concepts, I probably am going to disappoint you. For the average business, I don't believe most of those criteria add much to their strategy. Link building isn't about technical tools. It's about being valuable and interesting.

In short, if you are getting links from your industry leading sites, your peers and any site that relates to you in some way, you are getting the links you should be getting. You don't need a fancy number to tell you where to get a link.

How Do You See Links?

Numerous tools available online can help you see who's linking to your Web site.

Yahoo Site Explorer was once the main tool we all used to show you the links coming into any Web site URL. It allowed you to see what sites contribute to a competitor's current link popularity. But because Yahoo doesn't know what it wants to be when it grows up, they have gotten rid of virtually all of their search-related resources. I wouldn't be surprised if someday they dig up all that old stuff again. But as of now they just serve up Bing search results.

Today, my company, SageRock, is using tools such as SEMRush and Open Site Explorer by SEOMoz and MajesticSEO. Also Google Webmaster Central provides many great tools for understanding what Google knows about your site.

You can go to any search engine and do this search: link:www.yourdomain.com

That should show you who is linking to your domain. Unfortunately, we know that Google intentionally hides most links it knows about when using that search parameter.

There are other tools that will show you links to your site. Bing Webmaster Tools is also a good one. We'll talk more about these in the Tools For Analysis and Monitoring chapter.

How Do You Get More?

You can increase the number of inbound

links to your Web site in several ways. Some work well. Some used to work, but have diminished in effectiveness as time goes on. Some techniques that were once acceptable are now downright dangerous.

Here they are, warts and all:

Free Directories -- A multitude of directory and information Web sites offer free links. If you're low on links, directories offer a nice, quick fix. What directories can give you in volume, however, often may not translate into quality. Not all links have equal value.

Reciprocal Links -- Asking clients, partners, and strangers in related industries to link to your Web site and then returning the favor was a very popular tactic of the past. Now, most engines compensate for reciprocal links in their ranking algorithms. In other words, links exchanged between sites no longer have much value.

Buying Links -- Because reciprocal linking is mostly dead, brokers will help connect people to

Web sites willing to sell one-way links to your site. The sites offering link space are often valuable enough in the search engine's eyes to have earned decent PageRank. But the Google Penguin updates have shown that the long-term effectiveness of a link-buying strategy is questionable... at best. The ability of search engines' algorithms to detect and devalue purchased links will only increase and ultimately determine whether your link buying money is wasted. We now see a multitude of examples where buying links is not only wasted money but dangerous money. Google is aggressively flushing link buyers and sellers out of its search results.

Link Bait – This is a golden nugget of content on your Web site that encourages people to link to you. This "bait," when spread throughout different Internet hot spots, will tempt site owners to link to your site. Usually, link bait has a viral effect. Using link bait can be a good tactic to create volume (a large number of inbound links). In addition to volume, link bait can be good for the overall quality of your inbound links. Executing a link bait strategy, on the other hand, can be more than a little complicated. Read on!

Understanding Link Building

We have defined the basics, but what, exactly, *is* link building? This is my definition of link building: The integration of useful elements into a whole Web site to allow for the accretion of links through natural means.

In other words, building links is as much about having something to link to as it is about getting the link. Without one, you cannot have the other. Integration and accretion are the two elements of link building. Let's define and look at these two elements in closer detail.

The Element of Integration

Integration is defined as: The process of incorporating parts, components, elements into a larger defined unit, set, or whole. A site that does not have the integral or built-in components desired by its audience or its admirers (other site owners who potentially might link to it) cannot, by definition, engage in a successful link building campaign. This means that a site owner who builds his site solely from his singular perspective and does not ask and involve his audience within the process of development will, by default, build failure directly in the design.

A site with full integration addresses the needs of all audience members. This includes customers, employees, prospects, industry associations, and competitors. Each of these sets of people must be understood and addressed. By doing this, you give your site a significantly higher likelihood of attracting links. By leaving any of these users out, you are isolating entire segments of your online audience. This is incredibly limiting, considering that the complete integration of your audience members is still just a small percentage of the entire online population.

The Element of Accretion

Accretion is defined as: An increase by natural growth or addition. Without integration, accretion is impossible. This is why we see Web site owners delving into unnatural link building means. Without an integral site that addresses the needs of all audience members, buying links and engaging in link farms becomes the only option. Accretion simply cannot happen without integration.

Accretion manifests itself in two forms. The first form is through viral awareness. One audience member recommends your site to a Web user who then becomes a part of your audience. Standard mechanisms for this might be "send to a friend" e-mail components or icons for social recommendation sites like Facebook, Twitter and Google Plus. Links to such mechanisms simply should be standard architecture on today's Web sites. Not including these elements makes this viral recommendation strategy much more difficult for your audience, consequently causing an architectural failure within accretion.

The other form of accretion is standard public relations. You must make people aware of your integral Web site and ask that they link to it. In fact, letting people know about the integration you have created on your Web site without then asking them for the link is much less effective.

About asking for the link: I like this metaphor: *The honeybee moves pollen from one flower to another much more effectively than the wind.* Hoping for the link is much less effective than asking for it. Asking for the link, incidentally, does not violate the organic growth definition of accretion as long as other Web site owners are not given artificial incentives for the link, such as a quid pro quo or compensation.

By understanding the definition of link building, you can create a link-building campaign that is truly effective. Integration and accretion make up the law of link building. You cannot have one without the other. Together, you are assured a winning link-building campaign.

Integration in Action

Often in link building, people become so focused on obtaining links (accretion), they completely ignore what exactly they are going to have people link to (integration). This is the fatal flaw of link building.

Offer Something Special

One Christmas when I was very young, I had an idea for a Christmas present for my mom. I got a big box and filled it with my Matchbox cars. I then wrapped it up and made it look very nice. It seemed like a good idea. And sure enough, on Christmas morning, my mom was very excited. There was a big, heavy box. I was pretty excited too. But as she opened the box, I realized that this wasn't the great idea I thought it was. It was a hoax. It looked like something of interest and value. But inside, it was nothing. I wanted to give her something as special as that big box suggested, but because I couldn't afford much, I filled it with things I liked (not things she liked or wanted). In hindsight, I could have been more creative and staved off disappointment with a handmade gift instead of a pile of old toys.

Web owners do this all the time. We wrap up our Web sites in big, heavy boxes with fancy paper. But when someone delves into the site and opens the box, it's hollow -- no good or interesting information, nothing new, nothing they need. If a site has nothing to offer, the purpose of link building is moot. Maybe, like my childhood self, you think you can't afford something special, but I assure you, you can definitely find something special by being creative.

Search for Competitor Ideas

So, how do we put something of value in the

box? Start by getting the creative juices flowing. First, consider your industry. Type in the general key phrases that pertain to your site and see what comes up. The search leaders in your industry have almost certainly devoted both money and creativity in making their Web sites do well. The more competitive the industry, the more this is true. Let's take a look at a couple examples.

Start by looking at the top listings in Google for a phrase such as, '"financial advisor." When I last did this search, the first listing was Financial Advisor Magazine (not including Wikipedia). At the top of their home page, that site lists the latest Financial Advisor news. The next section lists the articles of the current issue of the magazine.

While I had never been to this site before, it was instantly easy to imagine that this site, indeed, is probably at least one of the industry leaders for all things pertaining to financial advising. If I was interested in this topic, I'd make it a point to bookmark it or sign up for an RSS feed.

Apply the Ideas to Your Site

If you are a financial advisor, what could you do to compete? Do you have a region you focus on? Do you have a specialty you focus on? Below are some ideas that come to mind.

"Financial advice for people who hate financial advisors"
"Financial advice for the poor and debt ridden"
"Generation Y financial advice – Not your dad's financial advisor"

As a general rule, the riskier an idea seems, the closer you probably are to a good idea. "The Financial Advice Forum" is not going to work. It's boring and has been done.

"Obsessively specialize. No niche is too small if it's yours." Seth Godin

Let's look at the phrase, "business

accountant." The top listing in Google when I last searched was businessaccountant.com. It has an extensive FAQ section that links out to individual pages concerning each topic. It has tax tips, again made up of individual pages discussing the tip. And it has foreign investor information, which then leads to its newsletter. Open Site Explorer shows it has about 1,100 pages on its Web site.

So, if you are a business accountant, what could you do? Again, think about your business focus and specialties. How about:

"The Bar and Grill Accountant. You make the food; we'll keep you out of jail."
"The Human Accountants. Is your accountant more cyborg than you'd like? We can help."
"Starving Artist Accountants. We love art as much as you do. We're just no good at it."
"Business Accounting Hell. The worst business accounting stories anywhere on the planet."
"The Subservient Accountant. Ask our

accountant to do anything day or night."
Incidentally, this is actually a fusion between
Trevor the Mentos Intern and Subservient
Chicken.

Integration Is the Key to Success

Remember, people go online for two
primary reasons: to be informed and to be
entertained. If you can combine the two, you are
really on to something.

Integration is the key to link building
success. But it is often glossed over. Ignoring
integration, however, pretty much guarantees
failure.

Accretion in Action -- Overcoming the Reluctance

I've yet to meet anyone who loves to chase down links. In my office, it's often who gets "stuck" doing links.

Some people outright refuse to do it. It's boring, tedious, and doesn't provide a great deal of intellectual fulfillment.

Getting somebody to do your link building for you would be a big relief. And if you could get somebody else to do your link building cheaply; that would simply be amazing.

According to a survey put out by Search Engine Roundtable, of 120 respondents,

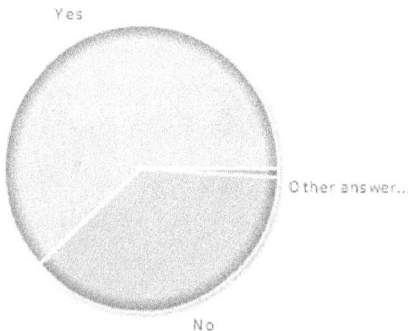

Yes

Other answer...

No

62 percent of them used interns for their link building. That's a lot of link building by people that don't know your business very well, and are likely to have never done any link building before.

One alternative that used to be popular is sending your link building to India and now the Philippines.

According to the Google keyword tool, these are the top 10 most-searched phrases containing the phrase "link building":

- ➢ link building
- ➢ link building services
- ➢ link building service
- ➢ seo link building
- ➢ link building india
- ➢ link building company
- ➢ link building strategies
- ➢ link building software
- ➢ link popularity building
- ➢ link building campaign

We all get a lot of spammy e-mail about outsourcing link building. With so many searches in Google for the phrase "link building India" and 62 percent of people surveyed passing off link building to interns, this leads me to believe that getting links is classified as a menial task. It's considered a necessary evil that anyone can do.

Re-Thinking Link Building

Ultimately, the problem begins in the vocabulary: link building. We're building links. There is no other goal other than that. Just build, build, build. And then build some more.

If 10 are good, 1,000 must be amazing. The phrase implies quantity over quality.

Google hates link builders. And link builders think so little of their craft that they're willing to outsource it to an intern or someone whose primary language isn't their own.

"Link builders" should start thinking of

themselves as public relations experts. After a company posts a news story on their Web site, then these online public relations experts try to get the story posted on appropriate Web sites, with a link back to the news.

I wish we could drop this whole "link building" phrase. It's becoming counterproductive for everyone. That said I'll be using the term "Link Building" throughout the book. Why? Because when snippets of this book are displayed in Kindle summaries, I want the link love. And people online search link building, not link accretion. I'm no hero. I have no plans to change the system to improve people's emotions about link building. I'd simply rather have the link.

Creating a Link Accretion System

So no one wants to do the accretion work. Perhaps after the Integration piece is in place, we will all find more willing accretion experts. And once we solve that problem, what do we tell the new willing recruit when they ask, "So how exactly do I go about this now?"

I put together a guide to starting a systematic, disciplined link building campaign. For those of you who've already started a link campaign, maybe you'll find some tips to help you systematize your process. For those who haven't started yet, print out the steps below and tape them up near your computer:

1. Make a Spreadsheet

Create six columns with the headings: Site Submitted To, URL Submitted, Date Submitted, Date Link Posted, Link Host Page URL, Notes.

In the notes section, keep track of how many times you submitted and any response you received from the site. You can use this spreadsheet for all sorts of links: directories, press releases, and blogs -- any place you submitted, posted or asked someone for a link.

2. Use Open Site Explorer

This is a great tool to keep an eye on your competitors. This tool will show you how many pages and how many links go to a Web site. Use this tool to get inspiration of where to find links. If a competitor has a link, maybe you can get it, too.

3. Have Something to Say

This becomes easier when someone running the web and marketing end of it understands integration. The site will be filled with news worthy content and the CMO will be sending memos to everyone about the offline and online campaign tie ins and connections. Those are the talking points to seed Internet hot spots for links. If those still don't exist in your organization, then find something going on that you can talk about. Is there a new service or product you just launched? Did you just hire someone? Did you or someone in your organization donate or volunteer in your community? Just write about what's going on with you and your company.

4. Submit to the Major Directories

Spend time reviewing the requirements of sites such as Yahoo, DMOZ, Business.com, and Best of the Web. Submit exactly as they suggest.

5. Develop a List of Industry Web Sites

Compile a list of blogs, information sites, and news sites that write about your industry (also, consider making this another tab in your link building spreadsheet). Use this ever-growing list of sites and contacts to submit news and information. Be personal and on-topic when you submit your news. Specifically ask for a link back off the news or article to your site.

6. Create a Schedule

Commit to writing a news piece in regular intervals -- once a week, twice a month, once a month. Stick with it. Submit your piece to the list of contacts you're creating. They won't come to you. You have to go to them.

7. Think Social

Consider making the news piece in print, audio, and video. Then get active in the online communities that matter to your company. If you aren't actively involved in the communities, you're lighting gunpowder outside of a barrel. You'll get a little explosion, but it's nothing like putting the stuff in a gun.

I know this is the case because of an experiment I ran a few years ago. Like many people at the time, I loved the show "The Apprentice." I watched it religiously, so I decided to blog about the entire third season. My goal was to be the best season three blogger.

I recorded every episode so I could rewind and get every detail. I almost dictated the show. I followed every nuance and innuendo. I linked to every sponsor company and special guest.

It was awesome. I know it was awesome because my visitors told me it was awesome. Sure enough, all five visitors agreed it was the best blog about the third season of "The Apprentice."

I was hoping to get visitors from good search engine ranking and word-of-mouth promotion. Sure, I had a decent search ranking -- I was in the top 10 results for "The Apprentice Season 3" -- but I didn't even rank for the phrase "The Apprentice."

I can't believe how naive I was. Did I actually think people were going to tell their friends about "this awesome blog about 'The Apprentice'?" Who does that? People go to a site they like and then leave. I rarely share a site with my friends because I'm not sure if they would like it, and they're super busy people.

I should have hung out at all the other "The Apprentice" blogs, participated in their comments, and contributed to helping make their sites better. In doing so, I could have occasionally mentioned my site. That would have been a huge help in getting more traffic.

After all, there were several much more established blogs. Some dedicated (insane?) people had been blogging about every season of "The Apprentice."

I also know from past experience that I get traffic from people who read my posts when I participate in online forums. Often, you can't promote your own site in a forum; however, you can usually link to your site from your profile.

As my kindergarten teacher used to say, *"If you want a friend, be a friend."*

Accretion Outside the Box

I want to share one idea that you can act on right this very minute to help you with your link building. It will cost you $25 a month. (But you're worth it.)

Here it is: Get a Ning account.

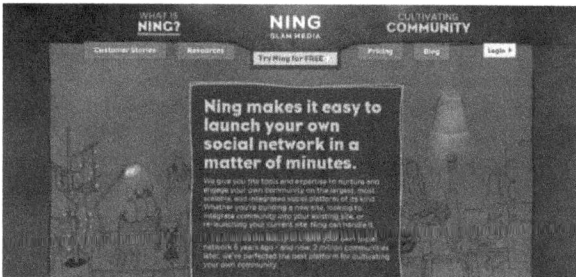

Ning is a private social network. It's a place that's all your own, where you can invite your customers and prospects to engage in a conversation with you about a topic of your choosing.

If you own a restaurant, you could have a Ning community about healthy eating in restaurants or places to go after dinner in your community.

If you're an accountant for small businesses, you could have a Ning community about changes in the tax code that affect your clients.

If you're Web designer, you could have a Ning community that looks at good and bad designs of companies that fit your target market.

The trick is to make it a topic that's interesting to your target audience. You don't want to be all things to all people. In fact, often the more focused you are, the better the community will be.

But you also don't want to have a community about something people don't care about. Namely, don't create a community all about your products and services. I'm sorry to say, but only you care about those. Start with a topic that addresses a need and then, when appropriate and not too often, remind the community that you offer a product that might help in a particular situation.

Ning makes it incredibly easy to set up a community. You should be able to set one up in about 10 minutes. Then you're pretty much open for business.

You can include things like:

- Photos
- Videos
- Blogs
- Forums
- Groups
- Notes

You can allow your community to be completely open so anyone can join it. Or you can make it completely private so only you are able to let people into it. Or you can do something in the middle.

Now for the downside:

Ning used to have a completely free account. It was regularly talked about in the news. It was a darling of the social networking world.

That's all changed.

While there is a 14 day free trial they then want you to fork over $25 a month.

It seems pretty steep to me. But the service is still good. For someone that is looking for a private social network this could still be a decent option.

I especially recommend pointing your domain name or subdomain to your Ning community. That way, it'll be branded nicely as your own site and get all the link juice!

See, I told you I hadn't forgotten about links.

The absolute best way to get links to your site is to have something valuable to link to. A community where you're helping people with issues or concerns they have is the prime example of "something valuable."

Once your community starts flowing (which won't be easy, incidentally; you'll have to ask people to join your community and be a major contributor yourself), you'll be able to easily go out to resource sites within your industry and ask them to link to your new Ning community. They will likely be more than happy to do so because you're adding value to the entire business community, not just your bottom line.

Look at how some of these Ning communities are benefiting from a link point of view:

These are all very niche sites discussing very specific topics. But they're getting a lot of people raving about their sites and giving them links for it.

How does this radically change your business, push you through tough times and make you a hip, new 21st century business? John Gerzema, "The Brand Bubble" author, gave us some insight during his Search Engine Strategies New York keynote presentation.

Gerzema said that businesses around the world are being hit by a major "trust virus." People don't trust anyone anymore. Consumers are now looking very closely to see which companies will offer them meaningful value in their lives. That's precisely where your Ning community comes in.

If you aren't into spending $25 a month on Ning you might consider the open source alternative: BuddyPress:

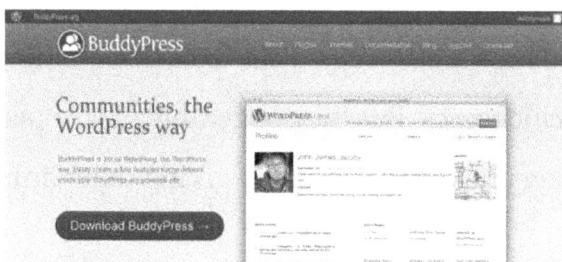

BuddyPress is a plugin for Wordpress sites. This is what they say about BuddyPress on their About page:

About

"BuddyPress was conceived in 2008 while working to add social networking features to a WordPress MU powered site. The first official stable release was in May 2009. The platform has grown and morphed considerably since then, into the dynamic, easily extensible package you see today.

Just like its parent project WordPress, BuddyPress is a completely open source endeavor. Everything from the core code, to the documentation, themes and plugin extensions are all built by the BuddyPress community. This means anyone can help the project by contributing their time and knowledge."

What can I use BuddyPress for?

BuddyPress is built to bring people together. It works well to enable people with similar interests to connect and communicate. Some of the fantastic uses might be:

- ➢ A campus wide social network for your university, school or college.
- ➢ An internal communication tool for your company.
- ➢ A niche social network for your interest topic.
- ➢ A focused social network for your new product.

It is definitely a viable alternative to Ning for creating your own social community. But you are going to be responsible for configuring it and managing it. If installing Wordpress on your own server sounds like a near impossible task, you probably would be better off just spending the $25 a month and going with Ning.

The Power of Sharing: Link Building in Online Forums

Participating in online forums is a great link building activity. You definitely can't be a blatant link spammer. You have to understand the policies of each forum. You also can't come into a forum and be aggressively needy. Never start throwing around links to your site in your first posts.

I also wouldn't recommend coming into a forum and asking for big favors right off the bat. I've seen people come to a forum and ask things like: "Please look at my site and tell my why I'm not coming up in the search engines."

That's a big topic. You'll often be kindly asked to spend some time on the forum reading and participating. So often, when I see a post like the one above, the person gets the information he wants and then is never seen again.

Like most other things in business, link building, is about relationship building. No relationship in your life has grown out of you just demanding help and attention. People will only be your friend if you give as well as take.

Forums: Long Term Accretion Benefits

This give and take has maybe never been more apparent than with the SearchEngineWatch.com forum moderator,

Nacho. Nacho oversees Multilingual Search Markets & Non-US Engines and Yahoo Paid Inclusion/Site Match at the Search Engine Watch Forums.

On Nov. 7, 2004 Nacho started the "Link Building 101" thread; a comprehensive to-do list for creating a link building campaign. If you read his first two posts, all you can say is, "WOW, What a lexicon of link building information!"

Nacho points out that he loves link building. This love clearly shows. You simply couldn't have the discipline and dedication to create such a link building resource if you didn't love the topic.

Another interesting thing about this post is that Nacho decided to post this information on his favorite forum. He didn't try to horde the information by keeping it on his own Web site or making it some sort of official white paper. Although he may have done those things, I didn't find his resource in those areas. I found it at the SEW Forums.

You'll also notice that nowhere did he say something like, "If you would like other really cool information like this, check out my site!" His post was all in the spirit of giving.

Not until October 2009 did they finally close that thread (who knows why. I guess good conversations should be stopped.) The common comments are things like how relevant his findings are to this day and how thankful people still are that he put it together.

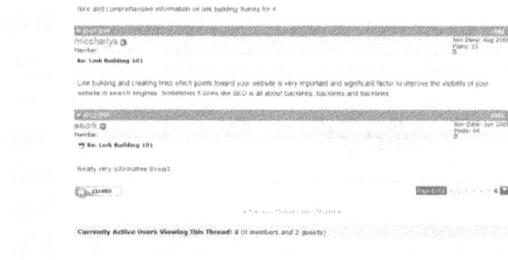

Keep in mind that all Nacho did was gather information. He didn't set out to be the next great link building expert. All he did was say, "Hey, check out these cool resources."

Granted, that's no small task. But he also wasn't reinventing the wheel.

More Posts = More Traffic

"So, nice anecdote, Sage, but how does any of this help Nacho?"

Good question. As I mentioned, Nacho didn't try to get anything outwardly obvious from this post. However, Nacho is a clever one. I highly doubt his intentions were purely altruistic.

You see, Nacho knows what all heavy participators in forums know. When you contribute in a meaningful way to a forum, people will take the time to find you. Nacho isn't just your mild-mannered SEW Forum moderator. He's also the CEO & Founder of iHispanic Marketing Group. iHispanic helps companies market to the U.S. Hispanic market and in Latin America. Nacho's full name is Nacho Hernandez.

"How do you know all this about Nacho, Sage? Are you friends with Nacho?"

No, I've never met Nacho. I know this because every time Nacho posts to the SEW Forums his name links to his profile. His profile has all sorts of information in it, including a direct link to his company Web site.

Now, I don't know how much traffic Nacho gets from his posts. He posts quite a bit: Total Posts: 1,385 (0.98 posts per day). What I can tell you is that as a CEO of a company, you don't do anything every day for years on end unless it pays off. When I'm even just a little active in forums, the traffic to my business site gets nicely padded from my forum profile link.

Now Nacho has received one more gift from a post he did so many years ago -- a link from me. Well-placed, good content can be the link building gift that keeps on giving.

There you have it, a chapter on link building by referring to a link building example that uses the topic of link building.

Giving Links Away

Since inbound links are the key to top SEO, people seem to forget that links don't just go one way. You could, and probably should, occasionally link out to other sites.

While you have no control over who links to you, you do have control over what sites you link out to. If you find yourself giving links to less-than-reputable sites, your search engine rankings could suffer for it.

There will be more on this topic in the Links and SEO section under "Siloing and Sculpting."

Content is King

Panel moderators enjoy asking questions like, "What is, in your opinion, the ONE most important thing we need to know about Link Building." When asked this, the answer from every panelist's mouth is the same. Content. The key to Link Building is developing the site Integration piece and the main component in Integration is content.

Just as the answer to the question is always the same, so is the objection. It goes something like this: "I make CNC machines! I can't make an Elf Yourself game! No one cares about this stuff enough to link to it." To this I say, "If no one cares then get off the internet. You're wasting everyone's time and bandwidth." I am not actually a jerk. My point is that every business has something worth saying and that content deserves a link. You just need the right content.

You Can Build It, but They May Not Come

Am I the last person on earth who thinks of that saying, "If you build it, they will come"?

In case you're not old, like me, that saying comes from the 1989 movie, *Field of Dreams*. Ray Kinsella, played by Kevin Costner, is a hopeful dreamer who builds a magical baseball field in a cornfield. Eventually, ghosts of Shoeless Joe Jackson and the other seven Chicago White Sox players banned from the game for throwing the 1919 World Series appear on his newly crafted baseball field.

While the concept is cosmic, strangely just, and inspirational, it's also crap. If you build a baseball field in a cornfield, I'm very sorry, but you are going to have to market the hell out of that thing. And you can't just build an inspired online marketing initiative and hope "they'll come." I know this seems super obvious, but I'm the link expert that created an Apprentice blog in a vacuum, remember? So, keep this in mind as you spin up your brilliant content.

Building Something worth the Link

More often than not, site owners don't build a brilliant masterpiece that will attract links and then simply forget to promote it. Instead, they pin their hopes on a mediocre, brochure-ware site for link bait and then also fail to promote it.

Business Basics Won't Do It

Just because usability is critical and most people are looking for business basics on a Web site, doesn't mean content such as your company name, product information, key employees, case studies, testimonials and photos of your facility are a scintillating read or link magnet. You won't exactly be knocked over with hordes of people begging to link to your site with this kind of content.

However, such a site is not without hope. There are definitely some places where you can submit a standard business Web site for grabbing a little Link Love. In fact, Justilien Gaspard wrote an informative article, *Link Safari: Gear Up for a Hunting Expedition*, wherein he revealed four great places to look for high quality links.

http://searchenginewatch.com/article/2048554/Link-Safari-Gear-Up-for-a-Hunting-Expedition

Industry Organizations – Almost every industry has one or more places offering membership and networking. Usually there's a member or resource page full of links.

Industry Magazines & Journals – Sometimes the organization above runs a journal, newsletter or other print publication. Get published. Get a link.

College Resource Pages – Are you in an industry people are specifically trained to enter? Then it's time to create a tool, whitepaper or other essential learning resource.

Government Sites – Most every library, city and government regulating body has a resource or helpful link section. You might think there's no way you can get onto one of these sites, but at one time NASA linked to nearby hotels.

As Gaspard says, "Approach each [of these] with an open mind."

Another good source for search engine directories can be found on Search Engine Watch. However, after exhausting the directory submission angle, you really need to create some compelling content or you're pretty much dead in the water.

How to Become Popular

First, let's think back to what the social scene was like in high school. Can you remember that far back? There were clearly some very popular kids and then some unpopular kids. While the memory of that fact may be chilling to some of you, the good news is that popular kids actually came in many variations.

It wasn't just the football players and cheerleaders who were popular. You had the funny guy, the lead in all the plays, and the student council president, who is probably still emailing you about the next reunion. Every clique had a ringleader. In your industry, you want your company to be the popular kid. You simply have to carve out your niche and ensure your Web site stands out as unique and special in your crowd.

Keep in mind that when people are spending time online they are typically gathering information or looking to be entertained. So as you consider ideas, think in terms of informing, entertaining, or doing both. Some companies tell me their industry is so boring there is no hope for them to attract links. Nonsense!

Making Boring More Compelling

Even a site offering the most mundane products can create compelling content. To illustrate this point, consider the following.

Q: How do you tell the difference between an extroverted accountant and an introverted accountant? A: An introverted accountant looks down at his shoes. An extroverted accountant looks down at your shoes.

See! Even accountants can be funny. A clever accounting firm could display the accountant joke of the week with archives of all the past accounting firm jokes. It could sponsor a contest for the funniest accountant joke or client story, and that might create a stir.

Maybe your company or industry *is* too serious to entertain. That's OK, but you can still be creative in the way you inform. A machine manufacturer could exhibit testimonials and case studies via video instead of print. With permission, they might even be able to go to customer locations to interview the people who actually use their machines or talk to the foreman about quality and productivity improvements while looking over the product in action. Wouldn't a customer find this 5-10 minute video more compelling than a four page print piece?

These two ideas were off the top of my head. When companies take the time to brainstorm while considering their target audience and market position; great link bait ideas will be born.

Just think about how you are going to integrate your audiences into your site. Don't you think doing a video interview of your customers will at least get them to link to your interview about them?

Make your site about everybody else and you are well on your way to making a link worthy site.

Don't Strive for Perfection

Perfect is the enemy of good enough. Social media is moving too fast to strategize how you are going to make your message look precisely the way you want it. By the time you figure out how to make everything absolutely perfect, your audience is going to be on to the next big thing. You'll never get a word in edgewise. Additionally, if you are too polished in your message, it stands a big chance of looking more like a pure commercial than something offering value to your viewers.

You have to move fast before everyone moves on. My kid never wants to watch broadcast TV. We either watch videos or YouTube. Right now, he's into animated fighting stick figures, but it's never a matter of what is being presented to him. For my son, it will always be, "What do I have the slightest interest in looking at right now?" Even though we personally accounted for at least 1,168 views of Rally's Rap Cat when my son was two, half of my readers will not remember that video and my son would no longer waste another minute of his precious time on something as silly as a rapping cat. (Actually, I'm going to go check that out again. It was pretty funny.)

Creating Link Love with Informational Videos

It's common knowledge in our industry that online video is underutilized. It's 2013 and that's still the case. People are currently uploading 100 hours of video to YouTube every minute. But in the business world it's a huge struggle to get a company to upload even one video. This is particularly the case in the B2B world where videos could create a lot of link love. Whether they are ready for it or not, the social media world is happening. In this world, your customers and prospects have the opportunity of talking about you in a very public way and completely without your approval. If you don't start participating in the social message, it is very likely that your corporate social message will happen without you.

Innovative Marketing Videos

Have you seen Will it Blend? A high end blender manufacturer uses video promotion to show users that its blender is the toughest out there. Is it really the toughest? I have no idea, but I know it blends cells phones and sneakers.

You might think you simply don't have the level of creativity needed to invent the "Will it Blend" of your industry. And you may be right, but you can do something.

The good news is that when it comes to information gathering, people don't need to be endlessly entertained. When in the information-gathering mode, they don't need or particularly want a bunch of glitz. They want the information they are looking for in an easy to access and understandable way.

In one of my earliest videos, "Search Engine Optimization Expectations," there is plenty wrong from a video-production standpoint. It's just my big head in too large a format. I could have cut away to other pieces of information. I could have spent a lot more time on it from a production point of view. But not one of the comments was about that. The comments were all about the content.

The great thing about video right now is that there is nary an industry that has a leader in this medium (except blenders). And so many industries could benefit from informational videos. I also have to say, it's incredibly fun. And once you have a system, it's incredibly easy.

Did you Say Content or Contest?

Being involved in contests, being a finalist in contests, and especially winning contests is link nirvana.

If a contest is anything, it's good content. Whether you win or lose, a contest has endless linking potential.

First, the contest itself will often give you a link. Sometimes you'll get a link for just entering. Sometimes you'll get a link for being a finalist. Almost invariably, you'll get a link for winning.

These links are often put on the home page of the contest Web site. Home page links are incredibly hard to come by, and are some of the most valuable links because search engines place so much importance and weight on home pages.

Additionally, your link will often be placed on a "winners" page that will stay on the site for years to come.

If you win, this gives you endless things to talk about in press releases and on your site. These kinds of press releases get picked up pretty readily. Of course, you'll have a few links pointing back to your Web site cleverly peppered throughout the press release.

Also, tell your vendors and customers about your win. They may link to you from their site. After all, people like being associated with a winner.

Even Losing has Link Potential

First, you aren't a loser. You are a "participant" or a "finalist." Second, you were in the company of world-class competition. "Just being a part of the process was an honor."

You'll want to put a page together on your Web site telling of your experience. Send out a press release to some local publications and any other places that might care that you gave it the "old college try." In fact, maybe your college would care. Or maybe your church, your chamber of commerce, or any other association you're a part of.

You can also go the "bad loser" route, if that's more your style. You could spout off about how you were robbed and how the judges wouldn't know quality if it smacked them in the face. These kinds of tirades are sure to get you a bunch of links, too. However, don't expect to be able to participate in the contest next year. If you do this enough, you might find yourself without any contests interested in your participation at all. But you might have gotten enough links along the way to warrant being ostracized.

Look for Contests Outside your Industry

Finally, don't get too focused on contests that are just about what you do as your primary services or product. There are all sorts of contests for all sorts of things. A four-person team from our office won the Muffin Day

Scavenger Hunt, which resulted in some decent links, as well as a year's supply of muffins. This was a contest put together by a local company celebrating their 20-year anniversary.

The name of the link building game is content. The trick is to come up with some compelling content. Contests are often just the content ticket you need to get on the link building train.

Maybe You Should Run a Contest

If there are no contests to enter in your industry, perhaps you should create one. "Really," you ask, "For my competitors?" Why not? Or it can be for your customers or for your primary vendors. Someone in your business world would enter a contest on your website – whether it's for $10K, an iPad, or a winner ribbon logo for their home page. And if people enter, they'll link. They'll link to the press release, the contest submission form, the informational video, and the winner's page.

Social Media Link Building Strategy – Does it matter?

If you've been following the world of link building, link building strategies in the social media space have been a confusing and often frustrating topic.

This is because the vast majority of websites in the social media world use what is called a "nofollow" tag on their links. Basically it tells the search engines to not give links any credit. So you can have a really great link on Wikipedia and it wouldn't matter at all as far as the search engines are concerned.

Nofollow was originally created by Google in 2005 to help stop comment spam in blogs. You can read all about nofollow in this Wikipedia article.

http://en.wikipedia.org/wiki/Nofollow .

Incidentally, this has always annoyed me. You see, I have just given Wikipedia yet another link that has link popularity value. And they give absolutely no value to any link outside of Wikipedia. This seems incredibly stingy and hypocritical if you ask me. The reason Wikipedia is such a powerful force is because everybody linked to Wikipedia. And now they won't share the love back. But whatever, I digress.

So, search engine optimizers have largely moved away from using social media in their link building strategies for search engine optimization.

However, this is all an evolving topic. What I mean is that the search engines are seeing social media as a place that can offer very legitimate and valuable information when it comes to links.

If a link is being tweeted over and over and over again, there must be something interesting there. For the search engines to completely ignore this information would be shortsighted and too absolutist.

And sure enough, Danny Sullivan teased out in an interview that both Bing and Google use signals from the social media world to influence link popularity.

You will definitely want to read the entire article – *What Social Signals do Google & Bing Really Count* -- if you're into this kind of thing. http://searchengineland.com/what-social-signals-do-google-bing-really-count-55389

But here are some of the cooler quotes.

Bing on Twitter: "We do look at the social authority of a user. We look at how many people you follow, how many follow you, and this can add a little weight to a listing in regular search results." (Google said that they do use it as a signal.)

Danny: "Do you calculate whether a link should carry more weight depending on the person who tweets it?"

Bing and Google: "Yes."

Danny: "Do you track links shared within Facebook?"

Bing: "Yes. We look at links shared that are marked as "Everyone," and links shared from Facebook fan pages."

Google: "We treat links shared on Facebook fan pages the same as we treat tweeted links. We have no personal wall data from Facebook."

Those are important because it discusses the value of fan pages.

At the end of the article Danny sums it up nicely. He writes, "In the end, it's clear that Twitter data especially plays a role in web search, these days. Who you are is being understood. Are you a trusted authority or not? If there's PageRank for pages, both search engines have a form of TwitterRank for people."

In his last sentences in the article he writes, "Meanwhile, retweets serve as a new form a link building. Get your page mentioned in tweets by authoritative people, and that can help your ranking in regular search results, to a degree."

So let's sum it up even clearer: Facebook fan pages and tweets from authoritative Twitter accounts matter.

There's also an interesting video posted on January 14, 2010 from Matt Cutts at Google. In the video he states these general principles: Google basically treats links the same. They look at how reputable a link is. It doesn't matter where a link is from.

A lot of the profiles at Facebook are not public so they can't index them. But if the profile is public then they can fetch the links.

"We treat links from Twitter, Facebook, .edu, .gov the same," he says in the video.

"If a link is private or it is nofollow then that would keep Google from using them for PageRank."

So does nofollow matter or not matter with

link building strategies?

Danny addresses this in the same article. He says that both Bing and Google get what is called the "fire hose" of data from Twitter. This is just the complete stream of data that comes from Twitter. The links in the fire hose do not carry nofollow attributes. So if there is a series of links pointing to the same article this would have value.

At this point things become fishy. So we have learned that the search engines look at the authority of individual people. And they also look at this "fire hose." But supposedly they don't look at them together. So if you don't look at the links from a specific person then what are you doing with the information?

It seems to me that we can come up with one of two conclusions. Either the search engines are in the process of figuring out how to use the links from the social media world or they haven't quite decided yet on the best approach.

Or they are totally using that data right now and are trying to keep us off the topic.

Getting Likes as a Link Building Strategy

On November 19, 2010 Bruce Clay wrote an article, *"Are Likes the New Links?"* http://www.bruceclay.com/newsletter/volume 85/likesvslinks.html

He writes: "Obviously, Google would like to find a better solution for determining trust and ranking than counting spammy links. With link spam winning, search engines are turning to signals received from trusted friends (Facebook Likes), reviews appearing in the LocalPack (7-pack local maps), and in referrals and sharing within social media as new sources for testimonials. By substituting what a user's actual friends like in the place of spammy links, ultimately what we see today as link spam will lose its impact."

This makes complete sense to me. It is estimated that 1% of the Internet population produces content. So a very small minority of the overall Internet community is vouching for websites by writing content that has links. This lopsided segment of the Web society allows for relatively easy manipulation of link popularity. It only takes a few well-placed links to significantly change the importance of a website online.

But, if social signals were put in place that would tremendously broaden the user-base of people recommending sites. While writing this book, Facebook reports that there are more than 1 billion active users. http://www.facebook.com/press/info.php?statistics

That is a massive amount of people. In the stats they go on to say that, "50% of our active users log on to Facebook in any given day."

There is a strong belief in the Internet community that people with valuable and important profiles in the social media world are less likely to abuse their hard earned authority by putting out spammy links. So, if these people link to something then it probably would be a strong signal that the link has value. Therefore, these links could be really useful in determining the value of an article.

There is just one problem, however. While Google can access the authority of Twitter accounts, Facebook does not readily allow Google to access that information.

Enter Google+

While Google+ is a place you likely don't spend a lot of time socially, you shouldn't underestimate its importance in the world of link building.

You would do well to click over and take a look at this chart:

http://www.marketingpilgrim.com/2011/07/g

oogle-chart-worth-a-thousand-words.html

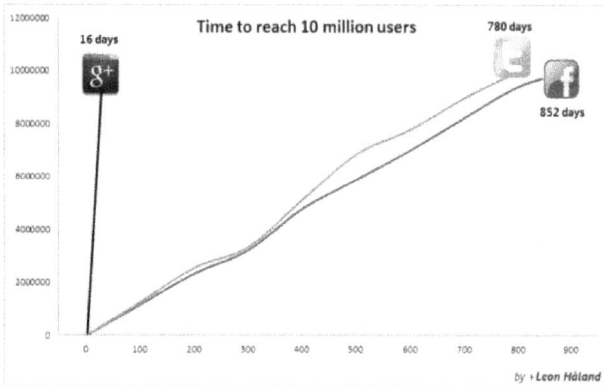

Image via Leon Haland

It took Google+ 16 days to get 10 million users. People are extremely interested in Google+. It remains yet to be seen whether or not it will be an important part of the social media scene.

But I can tell you this: changes definitely happen in social.

We know that young people are slowly, but clearly, moving away from Facebook. There is a lot of interest in Twitter with younger people today.

Yahoo bought Tumblr for over $1 billion.

Google continues to update and innovate at Google Plus. Counting them out of the game is not smart.

But whatever happens on the social front, Google is forcing businesses into it. Google Local listings are now Google Plus Local listings. They are integrating messaging into Google Plus. And most importantly, Google Hangouts. Hangouts are truly an innovative and valuable contribution to the online space.

There is also a lot of discussion on the use of author tags with Google Plus profiles. It is generally believed that having an author rich snippet likely doesn't have link value or contributes to the importance of an article. That said, we know without a doubt, articles with author tags get clicked on more in the Google search results. Why? Because people like pretty pictures. Articles that have an image next to them get clicked on more than articles that don't have a picture next to them.

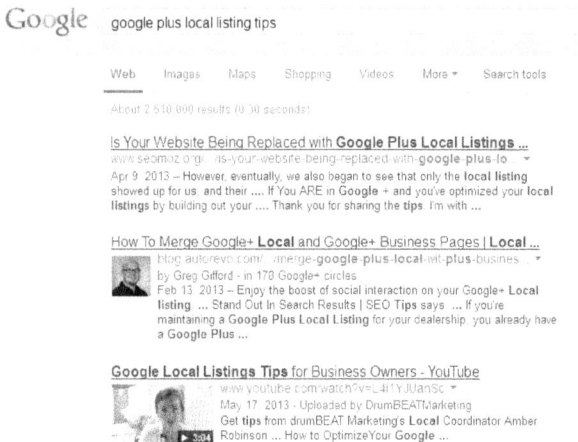

Without a doubt, Google is learning more about how people use the Web with information they get from Google Plus.

So you have now gotten to the end of this chapter.

What should you do with all this new found information?

Read on and I'll tell you...

Let's Skin This Social Media Link Building Cat

(That's my cat, Marty. He's too sweet to skin.)

Social Media Link Building Facts

There are a couple interesting facts regarding social media that are essential to know before social media link building.

- ➢ Important profiles on Twitter matter and are monitored by Google and Bing.
- ➢ Facebook fan pages are monitored and analyzed by Google and Bing.

> ➤ The "fire hose" of data at Twitter is monitored and analyzed by Google and Bing.
> ➤ Private information on Facebook profiles are not indexed by Google.
> ➤ Google states "we have no personal wall data from Facebook."

So, what are you going to do with this information?

Lucky for you, I'm going to give you some suggestions. There are many ways to skin this cat if you are one to like skinning cats. (What's up with that saying?) Well, since it's so visually intense let's get to cat skinning.

Social Media Link Building Cat Skinning Tip #1: Work on your Twitter authority.

There is a great article discussing this over here by Rand Fishkin -- *Google + Bing Confirm that Twitter/Facebook Influence SEO.*

http://www.seomoz.org/blog/google-bing-confirm-twitter-facebook-influence-seo

He gives some likely signals that would account for Twitter authority.

➢ Quantity of Friends/Followers
➢ Importance of Friends/Followers
➢ Analysis of Friends/Followers Ratios
➢ Topic Focus / Relevance
➢ Association Bias
➢ In a nutshell, get networking! Follow important people and work on trying to get other important people to follow you. There are many ways to do this. But some may include:
➢ Trying to engage with them
➢ Following them
➢ Telling them they are super awesome

You will have a much easier time getting more friends and followers if you are interesting on Twitter. I strongly encourage you not to promote yourself much, if at all. Just try to be a valuable citizen in the Twittersphere.

Social Media Link Building Cat Skinning Tip #2: Make sure you have a page for your company or organization on Facebook.

Facebook has recently redone their Facebook for Business section here:

http://www.facebook.com/business

They're trying to make it a little bit easier to make your way around that section. If nothing else, you are definitely going to want a Page for your organization. These are clearly being monitored by Google and Bing.

Again, be interesting! Don't make it all boring promotional stuff. You need to think of this as networking and not as advertising. Think about integrating all of your audiences into your social media: clients, customers, employees, vendors, community organizations. The guy that comes to the Chamber of Commerce meeting just running around stuffing business cards and flyers in everybody's hands is annoying. Don't be that guy at the Chamber of Commerce and don't be that guy on Facebook and Twitter.

Oh yeah, give away special promotions every so often. People like to "Like" Facebook Pages to get deals. So give them Facebook-only deals and incentives. They'll "like" you for it.

Social Media Link Building Cat Skinning Tip #3: Start to get comfortable on Google+

Make sure you have a page for your business on Google+. Make sure you've claimed your Google Plus Local listing (oh, you have one). Build out your local listing with pictures and descriptions. Encourage people to write reviews on your Local page.

Build out your personal Google Plus profile page. Make sure you have linked to your author page at places where you write in your Contribute section. Then link back to your Google Plus profile on your author page at those sites where you write.

Share articles you write on Google Plus.

Google doesn't talk a great deal about how it uses Google Plus data. But one thing is for certain: they use it. You have to participate at least a little in Google Plus if you are serious about your link building.

Social Media Link Building Cat Skinning Tip #4: Get Involved Already

I really recommend this article by Lisa Barone -- *Get Over Yourself & Build Your Personal Brand.*

http://outspokenmedia.com/social-media/build-your-personal-brand/

I hear all the time about how people don't have time and are not interested in social media. I simply do not see that as an option anymore. I'm sorry. I wish I could tell you something different. But I can't. Social media is here to stay and you might as well get used to it.

Just think about all the people that had to learn how to use the telephone, the fax machine, e-mail. The day they had to sell the horse to get their new Ford. I guarantee there was somebody that was not happy about it. We need to move on.

Your kids are on it, your niece and nephew are on it, your mother is on it, your boss is on it, everybody is on it. A billion people are on Facebook and YouTube right now. You are going to start to look silly.

As Lisa says in the article, "these excuses need to go die in a fire."

We all have something to sell. You need to build your personal brand in the social media arena.

Social Media Link Building Cat Skinning Tip #5: Keep an eye on Google Trends: http://www.google.com/trends

This is a great place to see what is hot in the

search world right now.

When you can, incorporate these trends within your tweets, Facebook fan page updates, blog posts, and Google+ updates. This is where people are searching heavily right at this moment. You can often times become part of that time sensitive conversation. This has the potential of driving a significant amount of traffic.

These current events are often times "trending" because they resonate with a large section of society. That means that it probably can affect your business or organization in some way. Don't be afraid to jump into that stream of conversation.

I recommend using the trending phrase exactly the way you see it in Google Trends. You will get better results that way.

There you have it. Five social media link building strategy cat skinning tips. No actual cats were skinned in the making of this chapter.

Link Tools for Analysis & Monitoring

You create the content, and the accretion tasks have been assigned to one or more "builders," now what? Well, now it's time for monitoring the success and tweaking strategy!

Website Resources

Part of strategy is understanding strengths. In other words, what good is link love if you don't know how many links love you? I want to talk to you about some of the places where you can go to track down your links. We are going to look at two traditional search engines and two blog search engines.

One of the easier things to do at a search engine is to type in the search box: "link:www.yourdomain.com." This, theoretically, should show you the links that a search engine knows are linking to you.

However, this has never been the case at Google. Google only shows you a sample of the links it knows about. So, doing this query at Google might only produce a few links, but in reality, Google might know of hundreds of links pointing to you.

Webmaster Central

To Google's credit, it offers a much more comprehensive link analysis tool in its Webmaster Central area. If you have never signed up for a Webmaster Central account, I strongly encourage you to do so. Google provides webmasters with information that cannot be found anywhere else. One such piece of information is the Links information within the Webmaster Tools section of Webmaster Central. It shows you, by page, how many links you have and who is linking to you. You can also download the information into a spreadsheet.

If you haven't setup your site in the Webmaster Tools section, I *strongly* encourage you to do so. All you need is a Google login. Then they ask you to either upload a page with a strange custom URL they give you or add some meta code to the <head> of your site. You can also now sometimes verify your identity with Google Analytics. Doing that verifies you own the site.

This gives you complete access to a ton of great information about your site. Not the least of which is your link information. The total number of links Google showed on their front-end search query for SageRock.com was about 42 links pointing into that URL. Open Site Explorer had 1,613. Google Webmaster Central has 6,617.

Additionally, Webmaster Tools nicely lays out how many links are pointing to each page of your site. Here are some of the results for pages on my site:

Your pages	Links	Source domains
http://www.sagerock.com/	4,283	597
/blog/	290	89

Your pages	Links	Source domains
/blog/title-tag-meta-description-length/	163	71
/live/	133	25
/airport/	100	3
/weblog/	78	35
/blog/key-phrase-research-strategy/	64	5
/blog/wolframalpha-not-google-killer/	54	18

Yahoo!

Yahoo played such an important part of link research for so long that I feel it's worthy of, at least, a mention. For years optimizers would use Yahoo Site Explorer to get a comprehensive report of link understanding. But the service stopped on November 21, 2011 and merged with Bing Webmaster Tools, which only offers backlink reports to sites you own. However, as a registered webmaster with a code for your website, other information and services become available, such as: submitting URL removal requests, dynamic URL rewrites, feed submission for Yahoo Search Monkey and more.

Marissa Mayer is currently the President and CEO of Yahoo. She has been pushing Yahoo in very aggressive ways. To date, her acquisition of Tumblr for $1.1 billion has caught the industry's attention.

Additionally, she also tried to get out of the Bing contract where Bing supplies all the search results and search advertising on Yahoo. She wasn't able to make that happen. But that doesn't mean it won't happen someday.

The 2010, ten-year contract apparently has language in it that may let Yahoo out of the deal if the partnership isn't performing.

By then the Yahoo search technology may be too old to salvage. It wouldn't be surprising if

Yahoo gets out of the Bing deal and then tries to make a deal with Google. It all reminds me of the strategic twists and turns of the Netflix series House of Cards. What if placing Mayer in Yahoo was a cunning strategy for Google to take over Yahoo? I probably watch too much TV. But you never know.

So, who knows. Maybe Yahoo Site Explorer will reappear as its own thing someday.

Third Party Services

If you are strategically and methodically building links, chances are you will want some tools to help you manage things. There was a great article put out in April 2012 from Search Engine Journal -- *15 Best Link Building Tools by Sujan Patel* -- that lists 15 Link Building Tools. http://www.searchenginejournal.com/15-best-link-building-tools/42129/

The ones in her list that I use include:

The SEOMoz Open Site Explorer -- I use

Open Site Explorer by SEOMoz for general analysis of links. It does a great job of showing me who is linking to a site and what the value of all the links are.

Raven Tools -- I then use RavenTools (which is built into The SageRock System) to organize my links for clients. It lets me easily catalogue links I want to pursue and then keep track of links once I get them.

The SEOMoz MozBar – Free extensions from Firefox and Chrome including a toolbar listing the key phrases in links, showing links that are "no-follow" & "follow" or internal & external.

Because of the Penguin updates, we've also been using Link Detox of Link Research Tools from Chris Cemper, which is not on Patel's list. It does a nice job of cataloguing your links by quality.

Patel lists lots of other comparable tools we've considered but not pursued such as Ahrefs, Ontolo, Tout and BuzzStream. For a full

list, read her article.
http://www.searchenginejournal.com/15-best-
link-building-tools/42129/

Also note, that I've used spreadsheets for
managing links. That works fine too. Whatever
approach you take, one thing is certain: you will
need something to organize your work. Not
having a management process is like not doing
link building at all.

Blog Search Engines

Let's start with blogsearch.google.com. This
is Google's blog search engine. Doing the same
query, "link: www.yourdomain.com," gets you
wildly different results. That's because the
results are coming strictly from the blog world.
These links are organized by date. You can view
the links you received in the past month, or in
the past hour. This is truly up-to-the-minute link
analysis. Further, you can subscribe to this
specific search query and have it sent to either

your RSS reader or your in-box via a Blog Alert
email.

Technorati

Another place you might find useful is
technorati.com. This search engine is highly
focused on things such as links pointing to your
Web site. Technorati refers to this as "reactions."
Try typing your domain directly into the
Technorati search box and view the information
it gives you. You can also create an account at
Technorati and then set up watchlists to track
incoming links to your Web site. These
watchlists can be imported into your favorite
RSS reader.

Downloads and Tools

James Bond would never have been the greatest secret agent on the silver screen if it weren't for his super-awesome gadgets. Fortunately for you, there are some great secret agent link gadgets that can make you a top notch linker.

Most of the best link gadgets you'll find are of the intelligence collecting variety. Intelligence is the secret weapon of any super-spy, or any SEO. The more you know, the more successful you'll be.

First, a warning about automated link-getting gadgets: while they'll promise you everything under the sun, they rarely produce meaningful results. This is because an automated link request invariably sounds like you've never been to their Web site and you don't know anything about what they do. Which is all true.

The number one way to get links is to keep an eye on what your competitors are doing. If you know what your competitors are doing when it comes to link building, you may be able to do something similar -- or maybe even do the exact same thing. The Web gives you the opportunity to easily examine what your competitors are up to.

Link Gadget No. 1: SeoQuake

You can see what the plug-in looks like here:

It tells you a tremendous amount of information about the particular page you are examining.

How many pages are indexed in Google? This helps you understand what you're up against with sheer amount of content. Content is king in the SEO game. If your competition has a lot more content than you, you'd better get busy creating some of your own.

How many links does SEMRush know about that point to that specific page, and also the overall domain? The quality and the number of links will give you a quick understanding of how you rate in the link building world. Here is the data that SeoQuake will show you about your site.

- ➢ Google PageRank
- ➢ Google index
- ➢ Google links
- ➢ Google cachedate
- ➢ Yahoo index
- ➢ Yahoo dir
- ➢ SEMRush links

- ➢ SEMRush linkdomain
- ➢ SEMRush linkdomain2
- ➢ Bing index
- ➢ Dmoz dir
- ➢ Alexa rank
- ➢ Webarchive age
- ➢ Delicious index
- ➢ Twitter Tweets
- ➢ Facebook likes
- ➢ Google PlusOne
- ➢ Whois
- ➢ Page source
- ➢ SEMRush Rank
- ➢ SEMRush SE Traffic
- ➢ SEMRush SE Traffic price
- ➢ Yandex CY
- ➢ Yandex index
- ➢ Yandex catalogue
- ➢ Baidu index
- ➢ Baidu link
- ➢ Compete Rank

Another great feature of SeoQuake: it displays its results in a search query. So you can instantly see all of the SEO metrics for each SERP. Such as:

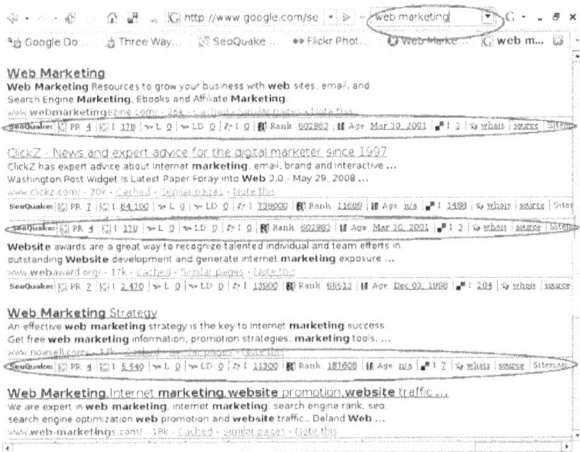

Link Gadget No. 2: Google Advanced Search

Perhaps you've seen a little tiny text link to the right of the search box at Google that reads, "Advanced Search." There are some hidden gems of spying gadgets in that area.

Within that page, there's a dropdown area titled, "Date, usage rights, numeric range, and more." Within that is a parameter you can pick called, "Where your keywords show up." This area gives you a dropdown selection where you can pick, "inlinks to the page." You can use this parameter for all sorts of sneaky things.

The best use of this slick gadget is to search on your competitor's name with the "inlinks to the page" dropdown box selected. This will show you links that have your competitor's name in the link. For added sleuthing, play around with the "Date: (how recent the page is)" dropdown. This will show you links that have been added to the Google index within a certain time period.

Link Gadget No. 3: Google Alerts

This tool is often used to keep an eye on what people are saying about you in the Web world. Don't stop there. Set up alerts for your competitors and important people within your competitors companies. You very well might find some announcements or recognitions that you could also get.

Master these three gadgets and you'll be one step closer to being the secret agent link sleuth you always wanted to be.

Why Monitoring Matters

Anything that is measured, will improve. That's one of the mysteries of the world. I recommend cataloguing this information. In a spreadsheet, or any of the tools mentioned earlier, keep track of how many links each of these resources are reporting. Monitor these numbers on a consistent schedule. You will likely enjoy watching these numbers improve and grow over time.

There are two added benefits to keeping track of all your inbound links. Watching this information will allow you to keep an eye on what the word on the street is concerning your site.

The first benefit comes if people are saying nice things about you in blogs or forums. You might be able to drop a line within these sites thanking them. Blog comments often allow you to include a link back to your site. So, you have the opportunity for another link to your site. While these links may be nofollow they could still get you traffic. Be careful when posting in forums that you know the forum's policy regarding links. Most forums these days are very particular about the kind of links they allow within their community. So, you might tread carefully in posting a link back to your site in this type of forum.

The second benefit comes if people are saying not-so-nice things about your site. These can be painful moments. However, you have the opportunity of joining that conversation and giving your side of the story. You can often post a comment or add to a discussion forum, letting the readers of that site know who you truly are.

Link love is a multi-faceted project. But if you have gone to all the trouble of getting links to your site, you should monitor the rewards of your efforts. You might find link love tracking to be one of the more fun parts of the process.

Links and SEO

The SEOMoz Search Ranking Report comes out every other year. It's a great analysis of what search engine optimizers believe are the most important criteria when it comes to ranking higher in the search engines. Report after report, it always says the same thing: Links are critically important. The kind of links optimizers think are important might change with each report. But having people recognize you with a hyperlink back to your site is crucial to optimization. Yes. You need content. You need great content. You need unique content. But if no one recognizes your great content, you will not be recognized by Google. It's really that simple.

In other words, link building is THE most important thing to do for high search engine placement. Having more links of high authority and high relevance is the dominating factor in

SEO.

So much of what is done in SEO is reverse engineering. Search engines won't confirm or deny much of anything. This is why I love the Search Engine Ranking Factors report SEOMoz puts out. The report asks top SEO experts worldwide to rate the importance of the algorithmic elements that comprise search engine rankings.

It serves as a good survey of respected industry people. It helps us isolate specific techniques and then see how the professionals feel about them. If you've never read the report before I highly encourage you to do so.

I want to detail three of the link algorithms given incredible SEO weight from all of these industry experts.

➤ Keyword Focused Anchor Text from External Links
➤ External Link Popularity (quantity/quality of external links)

> ➢ Diversity of Link Sources (links from many unique root domains)

Keyword Focused Anchor Text from External Links

For our examples, let's say our target phrase is "jay z tickets." As of this writing, it was ranked 57 on Google's Hot Trends list.

Keep in mind that uppercase and lowercase letters have no bearing on this. These variations will all give you the same results:

> ➢ jay z tickets
> ➢ Jay Z tickets
> ➢ Jay Z Tickets
> ➢ jAy Z tIcKeTs

However, these phrases are different:

> ➢ Tickets for Jay Z
> ➢ Jay Z Ticket

Several years ago we focused on getting exact match key phrases to link to us. So, in your desire to rank for "jay z tickets," you would ask people to link to your site with the phrase: Jay Z Tickets (or some capitalization variation of that). The easiest way to make sure this was done was to give people the HTML code exactly as you would like to see it.

Your e-mail to a potential external linker would look something like this:

"Thanks so much for wanting to link to us! You can link anyway you would like, but it would be totally awesome if you would link to our site with the phrase: Jay Z Tickets. Here's some HTML code for you, to give you an example:

<a href="http://www.i-love-jay-z.com">Jay Z Tickets</a>

And, if it's easier, here's a complete html snippet that you can just copy and paste into your site and be done with it:

Check out the greatest Jay Z fan site on the Internet! No one loves Jay Z more than these guys. Plus, you can get all your <a

href="http://www.i-love-jay-z.com">Jay Z
Tickets</a> right at the site. It's your one stop
Jay Z shop."

That is now considered a risky tactic. If all
your links (or most of your links) look exactly
the same, you are an easy target for Google. You
likely will be penalized for that strategy.

Today the best approach is to not give any
prescribed method of how to link to you when
you ask for the link. But that will likely decrease
your total number of links you get simply
because people won't know what to say in the
link.

The next best thing to do is to give people a
series of different ways to link to you.

> Tickets for Jay Z
> Jay Z Ticket
> Jay Z Tickets
> Misspellings would add to the
  authenticity:
> JZ Tickets

> ➤ JZ concert tickets for Cleveland

...you get the idea, right?

External Link Popularity

This is simply the total number and quality of links pointing to your site. You can track how many links are coming into your site using Open Site Explorer or Google's Webmaster Tools.

Open Site Explorer will help you catalogue your links by importance and authority. Not all links are created equal. Getting links from important people in your industry and region are going to help you significantly.

Diversity of Link Sources

That's probably pretty self-explanatory. Ten links from one site isn't as good as one link from 10 sites.

Today diversity is increasingly important.

> ➤ Blogs

> ➤ Forums

> ➤ Newspapers

> ➤ Twitter

> ➤ Facebook Pages

> ➤ Pinterest

> ➤ Press Releases

You want links pointing into your site from as diverse a set of types of sites as possible. If you have 1000 links pointing to your site, that all come from non-related blogs that no one else links to or comments on, you look like a spammer. And you probably are.

All Links Are Not Created Equal

I am often amused by link builders. They rarely care about the link at all. They rarely care where the link comes from or the value of the site that gives the link. They often don't look at the inherent value that a potential link might have.

They know they should be seeking more relevant, quality links. But that's hard. Because they were trained to get links in certain ways, it's not only hard it's nearly impossible for them. They don't know how else to do it.

Today I believe links should have inherent value.

Let's say you hired a public relations company to raise awareness for your company. They come into your office all excited after their first campaign for you. They show you a report of twenty places they got your press release picked up. The problem is you've never heard of these places before.

Your phone isn't ringing more. You aren't selling more.

They tell you not to worry. You want all of this exposure because it's going to help you down the road with the exposure you actually want.

I might be inclined to ask: "Why didn't we try to get some decent exposure that would translate into actual awareness that was useful to us now?"

If your new PR person was a link builder, they would say, "Well no one will ever truly care about your company. We're just going to trick them into looking at you once you're artificially popular. Then we'll see if they buy anything."

Welcome to the world of link building services. Buyer beware. Don't buy a service that's too good to be true.

If you are doing link building – hired out or

in house - only in hopes of getting higher ranking on Google, you are behind the times and missing the point.

Your in-house link builder or link building service provider should only be getting you links that will help your site directly. If you are having work done only to help your search engine ranking, Google will be able to detect that (either right away or eventually) and will likely end up penalizing you for it.

Get links that will get you traffic that want to buy your products. Ignore all others.

Something I've been looking at closely is how many page views a referring link has given me. I've found some surprising results doing this.

For example, while Google is still my number one generator of traffic, it definitely isn't the top generator of traffic that spends a considerable amount of time on my site. Discussion forums and blogs actually are best at generating traffic that sticks around. Let's look at some examples.

Source	Visits
google.com	40
clickbanksuccessforum.com	37
webmarketingwatch.com	29
marketingpilgrim.com	16
googleads.g.doubleclick.net	7
Youtube.com	7
facebook.com	7
wiki.answers.com	6
mail.google.com	5
click.ideo.net	5

The above grid shows some traffic that I received for a site. The numbers are organized by most visits to least visits.

Clearly, the winner from this perspective is

Google, which gave me more traffic than any other site over this time period. But let's look at that same data from a different perspective.

Source	Pages/Visit
marketingpilgrim.com	9.69
clickbanksuccessforum.com	8.89
mail.google.com	2.80
click.ideo.net	2.00
googleads.g.doubleclick.net	1.57
google.com	1.33
youtube.com	1.29
webmarketingwatch.com	1.21
facebook.com	1.00
wiki.answers.com	1.00

When organizing the data by pages-per-visit, Google is way down in the middle of the pack. By far, the top two sites that win this challenge are a blog and a discussion forum. Those same two sites also give me significantly greater average time-on-site numbers.

Let's look at another site. Here's the referring site data in standard form.

Source	Visits
help.twitter.com	86
images.google.com	53
google.com	38
facebook.com	31
searchengineguide.com	30
searchenginewatch.com	28
twitter.zendesk.com	15
searchenginestrategies.com	14
Stumbleupon.com	12

This one is interesting because Twitter is the number one traffic generator, rather than Google. Now let's spin the data around and look at it from a pages-per-visit ratio.

Source	Pages/Visit
searchengineguide.com	4.80
Stumbleupon.com	4.75
google.com	4.29
searchenginestrategies.com	4.00
searchenginewatch.com	3.75
twitter.zendesk.com	3.67
facebook.com	3.29
help.twitter.com	2.77
images.google.com	2.28

This data isn't as extremely different as in the previous example. But we can see that the top site that generates the highest pages-to-visit ratio is a blog.

But let's look at this one more way, from a bounce-rate perspective.

Source	Bounce Rate
twitter.zendesk.com	0.00%
Help.twitter.com	0.00%
stumbleupon.com	8.33%
images.google.com	9.43%
facebook.com	16.13%
google.com	21.05%
searchenginestrategies.com	21.43%
searchengineguide.com	46.67%
searchenginewatch.com	50.00%

Bounce rate is a guideline that gives you a feeling for people who don't stay on your site. The top three sites that have the lowest bounce rate are all social media sites.

These two sites are small samplings. I have access to sites that generate significant amounts of traffic. I'm not able to show the data here, but I'm seeing similar results with them.

You should look at your statistics this way. You might find some surprising results.

This is exciting because I feel like I'm able to have a direct impact on how much traffic I get from blogs, forums, and social media sites. As far as search engines are concerned, you simply have to try to optimize your site for particular phrases and then basically hope for the best.

But if you want more traffic from discussion forums, for example, then you need to spend more time participating in the discussions.

My clients often say that they don't need a ton of traffic; they just need the right traffic. By looking at the sites that give you visitors with high page view ratios and low bounce rates, you may be able to better focus on the sites that give you the "right traffic" in regards to links.

Siloing and Sculpting

An Allegory

Internal links are just as important to think about as external links. Lately, an awful lot of sites from really big companies aren't giving internal linking any thought whatsoever. Possibly you haven't taken time to think about this either.

Let me start by telling you why this is important.

Every page on your Web site has a coolness factor. Google calls this PageRank. But it could just as easily be called the cool-o-meter. It works just the way being cool worked back in high school. People were either cool or not cool based on who they hung out with. If you wanted to be cool, and you weren't already, you had to get a plan to beef up your coolness status.

I did this very thing.

Early in high school, I decided there was a group of kids that I wanted to hang out with. I had been spending all my time with a few skater dudes I'd grown up with, but they seemed to be going in a direction I didn't want to go.

One is now spending 30 years to life in prison. So I'm happy with my decision.

After breaking off all ties with my old friends, I began to dress different, got more serious about school, and became more outgoing. The majority of my sophomore year was a transition. I didn't hang out with my old friends, and I slowly made my way into the perimeter of this new group.

Then, finally, one day it happened. I was having a nice conversation with Suzzie (yes, her name really was Suzzie). She stopped me in the middle of our conversation and said she would be right back. She walked over to her clique; my hopeful future friends. After quietly talking with them, she came back and told me that she and her friends were having a party on Friday and she wanted to know if I'd like to come. In my head, I screamed a reply of, "HELL YES!" Then I told Suzzie, "Sure, that sounds pretty cool."

That was it. Everything was different from that day on. And everything else I did had a different air to it. I played the cello. That became cool. I got good grades. That became cool. I sang in choir. That became cool.

Until I met Suzzie, all those things I had been doing were unremarkable. Other than not skateboarding anymore, everything else was about the same. The difference was Suzzie and her friends.

This is exactly how linking works. Suzzie is your external link. She's hard to come by. And if you really want to hang out with Suzzie and her friends, you have to put in a lot of hard work and dedication. But once you do, then the things you do become cool, as long as you work them in right. The cello, grades, and choir are my internal links.

For example, one day I was hanging out with these people and I mentioned I had a regional orchestra concert. I was principal cellist. And if they weren't busy they might come check it out. The music would be good and the orchestra was good, too.

That's like putting a link on my home page to my cello. Because I was now accepted into the group, I just had to point out what was important to me. That then became important to them too.

Now, I was also a closet geek back in the day. I had a Commodore 64 and would code Basic programs on the weekend. I knew that would never fly with this group. So I buried it. I didn't bring it up. I didn't link to it.

I bet, however, that there are many parts of your site that you think are important but you bury them. Maybe you just link to them a few times on a weak subpage of your site. This will never make them cool. If you want them to be cool, you have to display them proudly all over your site. Think about all the places it would make sense to link to things you feel are important.

Every time you think about how to get a certain page better positioned in the search engines, just remember how it all worked in high school. If you follow that formula, you'll never fail.

A History: How Siloing and PageRank Sculpting was Done... Then

Controlling what pages of your site shared their link love was commonly done by adding a "nofollow" attribute to any link that you didn't want the search engines to give credit to.

Take the example Matt Cutts once gave. Maybe you have a friend who is a total underground, black hat, do-no-good, evil-empire, anarchist spammer. You know he's bad to the bone. But you have a soft place in your heart for him and you want others to check out his site. All you had to do is add a nofollow attribute to the link. It would look like this:

<a href="http://www.total-underground-blackhat-do-no-good-evil-empire-anarchist-spammer.com/" rel="nofollow">a black hat spammer</a>.

Matt Cutts was once quoted as saying, "There's no stigma to using nofollow, even on your own internal links; for Google, nofollowed links are dropped out of our link graph; we don't even use such links for discovery."

Now let's talk briefly about "siloing." Siloing was the idea of only linking out to other pages on your site and other outside resources that relate to that specific category or topic. So, if you had a cherry ice cream cone page, you would only link to resources discussing cherry ice cream cones. Information about chocolate ice cream cones and ice cream sundaes would either not be linked to or would be linked to using the nofollow tag like I showed above.

Controlling Link Flow Using Robots.txt

Link love was also blocked with a robots.txt file. This handy file goes in the root folder of your Web server and tells the search engines how to not spider and not index all sorts of things.

It can be easily created. In the first line, you specify what spiders you want to block from spidering your content. If you want the instructions to apply to all spiders, you can use an asterisk on the first line:

User-agent: *

You can also identify specific spiders to allow or disallow, such as googlebot, Yahoo's slurp, or Microsoft's Bingbot.

You can allow or disallow all pages using an

asterisk, or identify specific pages:

Disallow: /bad-page.html

Disallow: /terrible/yucky.html

Disallow: /really/no/good/page.html

And you can disallow spiders from indexing entire directories, like this:

Disallow: /cgi-bin/

Disallow: /yuck/

Disallow: /bad/stuff/

So, the end result of blocking all those files and directories in a completed robot.txt file would look like this:

User-agent: *

Disallow: /bad-page.html

Disallow: /terrible/yucky.html

Disallow: /really/no/good/page.html

Disallow: /cgi-bin/

Disallow: /yuck/

Disallow: /bad/stuff/

A word of caution, though. Unless you never want to see a spider come into your entire

Web site again, *never* set up your robots.txt file with this:

    User-agent: *
Disallow: /

That tells all robots to stay out of everything. I could walk you through how to do this in great detail, but, read on.

PageRank Sculpting Now: Then Again . . .

And then Google changed how they weighted links.

The basic gist has been, for some time, you used to be able to control how much value a link got by devaluing other links on a page. You did this using the nofollow tag on links.

You were saying, "Look, ignore Tom, Dick, Harry, and Rufus. Even though you see me hanging around them, don't give them any value. And definitely don't check them out just because of me. They need to get their cred from somebody else."

Now the rule is, "Just because you tell us not to give any weight to Tom, Dick, Harry, and Rufus, we don't care. We won't go check them out because you told us not to follow them on your behalf. But you're the one who's hanging around them (linking to them). So that's going to make other people you do want to represent less important. We can't be giving special props to who you tell us to. You're the one spending time with these idiots. Look, man, if you want us to think (this page) let's call her Sarah is so awesome, you need to stop spending any time whatsoever with Tom, Dick, Harry, and Rufus."

So, now "sculpting" is becoming irrelevant. You have two choices about your links:

Screw Google. You like who you like and that's the way it is.

Screw your link friends. Imagine Google is the hottest person at your high school and is dating you. Do you what they say, avoid the losers, or pay the price.

The other option is that you hang out with the less cool linkers on the sly... maybe across the tracks in a dark alley. You do this through iframes or JavaScript links that Google can't follow. You guys can all play "World of Warcraft" at some seedy gaming cafe out of the sight of your super cool friend.

In the end, I always advocate optimizing for the visitor, not the engine. But I have to take some kind of position on sculpting because SEO / Link controversy paints me and every other optimizer in a corner. If we don't recommend something, then we look stupid in front of our clients. If we do enact something, we look like sleazy optimizers that Google can say, "See! SEOs are just out to game the system."

This has made PageRank sculpting more of an issue. Not less.

I'm going to tell you to let the chips fall where they may, as I have done for my websites.

I only link out to sites I value. But if people are kind enough to post on one of my sites and links are allowed, I'll let them. My allegiance is to them, not Google.

Do Follow

Speaking of posting with links . . . Have you ever thought about using blog commenting as a way of generating links to your Web site?

You might think that it's relatively easy to go to any number of blogs and simply write a quick comment with a link to your Web site. This actually used to be the case. Consequently, blogs were often inundated with tons of blog comment spam.

To counteract this, most bloggers have made all comments "no follow." This means that, even though you can put a link in your comment on a blog, the link is given no weight by the search engines (although you may be diluting the blog's PageRank [see above]).

As an example, WordPress blogs default to all comments being "no follow." So if you install a WordPress blog and don't make any modifications, any links people post in your comments section won't get any value from a search engine perspective.

This really doesn't matter. A blog that is well read and commented on often will generate a nice amount of traffic for you. But this is only the case if you add relevant, on-topic comments to the blog post.

Any links you put in these comments must be valuable and useful to the readers. Simply spamming the comments of blogs will generate nothing for you and will probably get you banned from commenting on that blog again.

But there are also blogs that aren't "no follow." The comment links pass all weight given to them on that page. These blogs generate traffic to your site by the readers of the blog, and can also give you some extra value in the eyes of the search engines.

Some directories actually have been created that promote these kinds of "do follow" blogs. This has all become a bit of a movement. So, if you're looking to generate links that help you in the search engines by participating in blog comments, look at some of these "do follow" blog directories. There are also handy ways of seeing which blogs are "do follow" or "no follow" using a Firefox or Chrome browser add-on. Just look around for no follow plugins and extensions and you'll find one.

For example, comments in "The New York Times" appear to be "do follow." People utilize this regularly.

Look at regular "The New York Times" commenter D. Gundun. His links all work in the comments of the actual article he participates in. Further, we can see that Google is referencing these comments (and comments he does at other periodicals) by looking at what links Google gives him credit for.

Google won't show us all the links they have on record for his blog, but Google clearly indexes and follows the links he has put in the comments.

It's important to mention that his blog relates to the topic at hand. Don't spam "The New York Times" under any circumstances. However, you can offer links that are on-topic and useful.

I found this by using the Firefox add-on that shows which links are "do follow" or "no follow." Spending some time examining the capabilities of various blogs you might come across some that relate to your topic and also allow you to pass links value within your comments.

If you support this kind of thing, and you have a WordPress blog, you can add this "do follow" capability using plug-ins.

Paid Links

This is a very popular topic. It's got a nice magic-fairy-dust, solution-to-all-your-problems feel to it. There have been a lot of companies (mostly affiliate marketers) that have managed this environment successfully and experienced amazing results because of it. I believe their stories cry out like Sirens from a rocky shore. It's a tricky, potentially fatal environment. One most should not dare to tread. Why is that? Panda and Penguin, of course!

With all of the talk of the Google updates inflicting massive damage to sites caught inflating link popularity, you would think the link buying industry was dead.

But it's not. In 2013, you can easily find link buying networks at any of the search engine tradeshows. And they will tell you flat out that it's OK to buy links or to pay bloggers to post about your product all in the vein of increasing your link popularity value with the search engines. Nothing could be further from the truth.

Google is publicly admitting to removing thousands of link networks whose sole purpose is to get you artificial links for a price.

Google Executive Matt Cutts, talked about the changes sweeping through Google. Everyone is always dying to know – what's coming next and will it affect my website?

The Crackdowns: In regards to Penguin 4, Cutts basically said it's Penguin on steroids - more of the same with more of the same results for typical offenders. Paid content used to gather links, often called advertorials, will be getting attention too. The negative kind. Google also plans to continue cracking down on link networks and spam queries.

But it's not all about hand slapping. Google is working on rewarding the ones doing it right.

They want more sophisticated link analysis, which can spell doom for black hats, but is good news for those building genuine resource links -- especially if you're an authority in your industry.

Sometimes, there's a clever guy in a basement with an old domain and a link from CNN. Even though said dude has .00000047% of industry market share, he ranks #2 on page 1 for an important industry term. Google aims to help improve link algorithms to help product and service leaders get better representation, when they deserve it, over this guy.

Cutts says, however, this doesn't mean the big guy will rule the whole front SERP page either. Google will be looking for dominant domain clusters in SERPs and breaking them apart for more diversity on the front page.

Why Can't I Just Buy a Link?

Everyone is so focused on where the next

link is going to come from; they forget why they were supposed to be getting links in the first place. Let's back up and review why link manipulation is bad for everyone.

Before Google...

Before Google, the big search engine was AltaVista. It still exists, if you want to go check it out for fun. It says it's a Yahoo property, which means that the search results are coming from Bing.

Clients would come to me myopically focused on AltaVista. They just wanted to come up for their major key phrases in AltaVista. If they weren't successful in AltaVista, the whole campaign was a failure.

It's pretty funny thinking about it now. But it was painfully serious at the time. There were two reasons people stopped visiting AltaVista: old results and poor relevancy. AltaVista took forever to update its search index. And, when they did update, the results were not particularly great.

Link Popularity

Along came Google. Why was it successful? When you typed in a search query, the results you got were great. You quickly found what you were looking for. You loved it, and you told your friends about it. Google didn't need to advertise. Google was so good at doing what it did; it changed the face of search by creating the largest viral campaign in history.

You know why Google was so great, right? It was because its algorithm relied heavily on link popularity. The Web sites that linked to you gave Google great insight into what you were about and how important you were in the Web landscape. Google also did a great job of refreshing its index on a regular basis.

From Wikipedia: "By the end of 1998, Google had an index of about 60 million pages.[15] The home page was still marked 'BETA,' but an article in Salon.com already argued that Google's search results were better than those of competitors like Hotbot or Excite.com, and praised it for being more technologically innovative than the overloaded portal sites (like Yahoo!, Excite.com, Lycos, Netscape's Netcenter, AOL.com, Go.com and MSN.com) which at that time, during the growing dot-com bubble, were seen as 'the future of the Web,' especially by stock market investors."

So, poof, Google now has roughly 60 percent of the U.S. search landscape and oftentimes a much greater portion of search share in other countries. And why? Because they learned how to measure valuable links. And they're still learning and improving how they measure valuable links.

Getting valuable links has always been about getting recognized and ranked for good content. That, in turn, made search results relevant. Your Web site is part of a relevancy ecosystem. Paid links pollute that ecosystem and that eventually hurts everybody.

Paid Links: Seller Beware

There are two parties involved in this pollution, and it's not just buyers getting tagged and punished. There was a panicked discussion thread at Google Webmaster Help forums recently. The person who initiated the discussion wrote:

"Today I found that my entire site has dropped out of site in search results. I have a site that received over 2,000 search visits per day and today that has stopped."

Apparently, he had a bunch of affiliate links on his site. These are links to other sites that he would make money on if someone clicked on the link and bought something on the affiliate site.

Google employee John Mu jumped into the conversation:

"I browsed your site's reviews a bit and most of the links are either affiliate links or links to the companies without nofollow. This doesn't seem to match your reply regarding the use of nofollow. Perhaps it would be good to double-check and submit a reconsideration request should you find something that could be improved."

With this in mind, and just for the record, it's a good time to refresh your memory on the Google Paid Links policy.

Buying or selling links that pass PageRank violates Google's Webmaster guidelines and can negatively impact a site's ranking in search results.

It appears that the person in this discussion post got in trouble for not adding nofollow attributes to these, what are essentially, paid links.

The primary way to solve this problem is by making these links nofollow. There's a lot of confusion about what this means and how to apply it to your own links. So, let's look closer at the nofollow attribute so we're all clear on the topic.

Nofollow is an HTML code you insert into a link that lets the search engines know that you don't want them to crawl through this link or give it any credit that you were linking to it.

A normal hyperlink looks something like this:

<a href="http://www.example.com/">Anchor Text</a>

That is a standard link and tells the search

engines to crawl that link, find the content and, in the case of Google, share some of the PageRank from your page with this new page.

Because Google's algorithm depends on linking, this kind of link has become quite a precious gift. If you link to a site with this kind of standard link, you're telling the search engines, "Here is a page I want to tell you about that is really great. I'm getting nothing from this other than the warm fuzzies that I'm sharing, with you and the world, a great Web page."

If you link to a page because there is some quid pro quo, then you probably should think about adding nofollow.

It's easy enough. Your hyperlinks would look something like this:

<a rel="nofollow" href="http://www.example.com/">Anchor Text</a>

You probably should link to the page with the nofollow tag if you're getting money, a gift, or testing a product or service.

This also would apply to content that you can't vouch for. Say, for example, you have a blog and you allow commenters to post links in their comments. If you don't know what that content is, you probably should nofollow it (most blog comments are automatically nofollowed, but double-check to be sure).

If you're concerned about losing your Google ranking, take a moment and think about whether you have any links off of your site that you're either getting paid to have or could get paid if a certain action occurs on that site.

Negative SEO

There has been increased concern about "negative SEO." This is the practice of buying a large amount of links and pointing them to your competitor's site. Because Google is on the lookout for sites that have low quality and paid links pointing to a site, theoretically, you could damage the SEO reputation of a company's site using this strategy.

You can definitely find companies offering negative SEO. But this is an extremely seedy world. For all we know Google has set up a sting for people attempting to do negative SEO on a competitor.

While blatant negative SEO gets lots of press, the real concern I see is underground black hat SEO – unknowing companies getting links bought for them by their SEO firm. They don't know the tactic exists and think their SEO firm just "knows their stuff" and has gotten good results for them "somehow."

I've seen many cases where people come to us after experiencing a severe loss in traffic that turns out to be a Penguin penalty. They swear to us that they have never bought a link in their life. But with some minor digging we learn that indeed they have bought many links.

I truly believe they didn't know links were

being bought on their behalf. Their SEO company was doing this sometimes for years as an optimization strategy. That's how they increased search rankings... by buying links.

And then the client is faced with hundreds or even thousands of links pointing to their primary domain. How do you unwind that? How do you get all those sites to take those links down?

Breaking the link on your site could work. Except you can't take down your home page. It's impossible to make www.yourcompany.com a 404 error page. Most of these links are, of course, just pointing to your root domain.

So what do you do? I think, unfortunately, it's sometimes hopeless. While you try to repair your site as best you can, you probably should give serious thought to starting over. Set up a new domain with new content and new, quality links. It's a process that will take years. But it might be your only hope.

Don't Buy Links | Buy Exposure & Get Links

I love and highly recommend the article --
SEO Link Building ALERT! Paid-Organic Social Content Distribution Is The Future -- from Marty Weintraub of AimClear.
http://www.aimclearblog.com/2013/05/20/why-seo-link-builders-are-dead-without-paid-organic-social-content-distribution/

Do yourself a favor and read the whole thing.

In summary, he says: "In this post-Penguin & Panda link building environment, many old methods don't work anymore. As we link builders seek new age replacement methods, we're after content and distribution programs that:

> ➤ Earn real links from sites with good domain authority

> ➢ Generate authentic social signals from real users of good authority
> ➢ Insulate our sites from harsh search engine algorithm updates
> ➢ Drive targeted & scalable social psychographic traffic to content that converts
> ➢ Amplify PR distribution to journalists, bloggers, and a myriad focused media-role users."

He goes on to say that these "content distribution" platforms exist through the advanced targeting options on social media websites and advertising networks. So, in other words, you can still pay for links by paying to put your link worthy content in front of the right audience. Ideally the ones ready, able and willing (dare I say, excited) to link to and source your fabulous content.

While the obvious link buying techniques

are out, the old PR strategies of getting in front of influencers still exists.

I like the term, "seeding," for this concept. Ever break a potted plant that needs a bigger pot? There's a network of roots tangled up, which when teased apart and given soil, create a strong base for the upward growth. The seeds sprout, grow down, and develop into root systems. If you want your promotion to take root and stay strong, buying exposure and growing links organically can help develop that root system.

First you need:

<u>Soil:</u> Collaborate with the client to develop a hot online promotion.

<u>Pot:</u> Create a special microsite on the main URL with a double-dotted domain to support the promotion.

<u>Seeds:</u> Plant them through multiple channels and efforts such as:

Facebook Pages, Tumblr blogs, Twitter accounts,

Pinterest accounts, etc. – Think of it as fan invite and build out; regular fan communication and commenting.

This link seeding takes no money, but lots of hard work. The links are going both ways in this example, but this tactic is mostly reaching out with something interesting to say and knowing some sweet social media link love will follow.

Blog Seeding Campaigns -- Create an opportunity in third party blog advertizing conglomerates with nofollow tracking URLs. <u>They must be nofollow.</u>

Set the parameters, check the posts, and let her loose. With many conglomerates, a mini-community of sorts is being created with a built-in referral system that pays bloggers for both blogs and referrals and interactive widgets are embedded on blogger Web sites to help your promotion:

> ➤ Pop out of the content.
> ➤ Promote the built-in

interaction/community.

> Promote the Promotion itself to other bloggers and readers.

Water: Time to moisten those seeds with some brand reinforcement:

Social Media Banners like Facebook Social Ads – These ads should lead to the social media pages and the micro-site. Get the impressions and links your content needs with social advertising so the target audience sees the message that magic number of times needed to take action.

I cannot say this enough, DO NOT FORGET that all paid links to your site MUST BE nofollow. This is crucial. You will definitely want to check your links coming in to your site to make sure this is happening.

Paid Search Ads – Buy ads that lead directly to the micro-site. These are viral reinforcements. This is less about brand and network and more about pulling bodies into the promotion. It's that final morning mist that keeps the promotion fresh and green.

Newsfeeds – This is about buying your way into the newsfeed of people that will potentially write about you organically.

While Facebook, LinkedIn and Twitter advertising is a whole other topic outside of link building, you should know that you can target specific kinds of people in really powerful and fairly creepy ways.

You certainly could target editors, prominent bloggers and other influencers in social media advertising. If you had their emails addresses, phone numbers or Facebook ID's you could customize audiences using Facebook Power Editor. You could then pretty much guarantee that these people would see every press release and important happening at your company in Facebook.

You could also retarget these people using AdWords retargeting or a network like AdRoll for people that came to your "Press" section of your site. So, if a person came to your press section you could then serve ads in various ad networks and exchanges promoting your newest products and good deeds you are doing.

It's quite possible these people would see your ad that was specifically targeted to the press. You then might get picked up and written about with a quality link that counts in your link popularity score.

And of course, if you bought an advertisement in a blog or newspaper you significantly increase your chances of getting them to write about your in a featured story.

Well, I killed a metaphor today, but I hope you learned something about buying exposure for links. Now you know. You too can have a green thumb when planting a viral promotion.

Google Hates Crappy Links - Panda and Penguin In Depth

A story of links would not be complete without talking, in depth, about the Penguin and Panda updates.

First, the history:

In February 2011, Google made a change to its algorithm that became known as Google Panda. The goal was to lower the rank of "low-quality sites." Google said that it affected about 12% of all search results.

Updates to Google Panda have been coming consistently ever since.

In December, 2011, Kristi Hines wrote for Search Engine Watch: "Google Panda Update: Say Goodbye to Low-Quality Link Building."

She points out how Google penalized

JCPenney, Forbes, and Overstock.com for "shady" linking practices. It was uncovered that all three of these companies were acquiring low-quality links.

On January 2, 2012, Aaron Wall wrote at SeoBook: "This Post is Sponsored by Google."

Aaron discovered a series of blog posts that Google Chrome bought as a paid link building campaign. "Some of those sites are paid posts and have live links in them to Google Chrome without using nofollow."

Matt Cutts, Google's head of webspam wrote:

"In response, the webspam team has taken manual action to demote www.google.com/chrome for at least 60 days. After that, someone on the Chrome side can submit a reconsideration request documenting their clean-up just like any other company would. During the 60 days, the PageRank of www.google.com/chrome will also be lowered to reflect the fact that we also won't trust outgoing links from that page."

And then in April 2012, Google Penguin hit.

Microsite Masters operates a rank tracking tool. They took the data across sites that they check search rankings on to see if they could find commonalities among sites that got hit with the Google Penguin update.

They wrote a post on May 2, 2012 "Penguin Analysis: SEO Isn't Dead, But You Need to Act Smarter (And 5 Easy Ways to Do So!)" highlighting their findings.

Their overarching findings were that Google was trying to discover links that were "over-optimized." This means sites that have an over abundance of links pointing to their site that have the exact same anchor text.

They write: "More specifically, we were interested in seeing what percentage of those links had anchor text for keywords that the site was trying to optimize SERP visibility for (such as "blue widgets") versus any other type of anchor text (this could be "bluewidgets.com", "blue widgets | the number one widget site", "click here", or anything that wasn't a keyword containing measurable search volume)."

What they found was that "every single site we looked at which got negatively hit by the Penguin Update had a "money keyword" as its anchor text for over 60% of its incoming links."

They also found that "penalized sites generally had very little links coming from domains and websites in the same niche."

This is so interesting because these are blatantly clear behaviors of someone who has bought links. Artificial link building looks artificial.

On the May 3, 2012, Google Analytics Blog, Google announced that "now you can see all the backlink URL's, post titles, and more right within the new Social reports [within Google Analytics]."

To see it, go to Google Analytics, under Traffic Sources > Social > Pages and then click on a specific page.

Google writes, "If only you could crawl the web and build an accurate link graph. The good news is we already do that at Google, and are now providing this insight to Google Analytics users."

Google often times gives us access to the tools they use for analysis. Links are a huge target for Google these days. They are doing everything in their power to make the search results as relevant for the searcher as possible. Targeting sites that get links from low quality, irrelevant sites is an easy way for Google to do this.

And then there's always the good old way of having other webmasters do the work for Google.

Google Webmaster Tools has a comprehensive spam reporting page where you can report a wide variety of spam you find online.

In May 2013, Penguin 2 was released.

Matt Cutts tweeted a link to easily report spam Google may have missed.

Matt Cutts @mattcutts   23 Ma

In case you missed it, we're taking Penguin spam reports at bit.ly/penguinspamrep... and digging into the feedback we get

Collapse ← Reply ⟲ Retweet ★ Favorite ••• More

93   33
RETWEETS   FAVORITES

5:13 PM - 23 May 13 · Details

That link leads to here:

Google **Penguin Spam Report**

If you see a spam site that is still ranking after the latest Penguin webspam algorithm, please tell us more about it.
* Required

What's the URL for the spam site?
Address of the specific webpage that is spamming

What's the Google search result URL that demonstrates the problem? *
Copy and paste the Google search URL from the address bar

Any additional information about this spam result? *
If you know anything else about the spamming site, feel free to tell us here.

[Submit]
Never submit passwords through Google Forms.

On Wednesday, May 29th, 2013, Glenn Gabe at G-Squared wrote this article: Penguin 2.0 Initial Findings – A Deeper Update, But Not

Broader
[Analysis]:http://www.hmtweb.com/marketin
g-blog/penguin-2-initial-findings/

In summary, he says, that while Google could have used this opportunity to broaden their smack down of different black hat SEO, they are still, for the most part, going after the spammy inbound link. While they used to look primarily at inbound links to home pages, they're now going further into website directories to analyze incoming links.

In his own words, "When analyzing unnatural links of sites hit by Penguin 2.0, did the types of unnatural links change at all? Not from what I can see. I saw many familiar link types, including comment spam, article sites, spammy directories, blogroll links, link networks (public and private), etc. Basically, the same types of link manipulation are being targeted by Penguin 2.0 as were targeted by Penguin 1.0 (based on my analysis)."

Our company has had the opportunity to audit and work on sites affected by the Penguin updates. We see the same thing as Gabe.

Interestingly, we've often been presented with sites that the owner says is completely clean of low quality links. We then quickly find out that's not the case. They then come clean with the tactics they've used.

If you've seen a significant loss in traffic on April 24, 2012 or May 22, 2013 you very likely were hit by the Penguin update. And you very likely got hit because of too many low quality links pointing into your site.

The good news is: we seem to be able to repair this issue. It's not easy but it can be done. The process involves three parts:

➢ Requesting low quality links be removed.

➢ Disavow low quality links that you couldn't get removed.

➢ Increase high quality, industry-related links pointing to your site with a wide variety of anchor text.

It's not a quick fix. It takes patience and dedication. But it does seem to work.

Links in Action: Case Studies

Do as I say, not as I do. Yeah, that never works. Here are the real life examples of companies doing Link Campaigns on purpose or accidentally, while either succeeding or failing miserably.

Dogster & Catster Facebook Application

For this book, I invited people to submit sites they felt deserved a little love. Today, we'll look at some of these sites and discuss different ways to create link love.

I got a link from a friend about a new application created by Dogster.com and Catster.com; sites dedicated to the people who love their pets. You can share pictures, stories, and all kinds of information about your dog or cat. This new application allows you to embed adoptable pets or cute pet pictures automatically into your Facebook account. You simply go to the Dogster & Catster Facebook Application page and select the Facebook application you wish to embed. It will automatically install, quickly and easily, showing adoptable or cute dogs and/or cats.

This is a great tool to help rescued animals, and also a great tool to promote Dogster.com and Catster.com. The application defaults to a link in your left hand navigation for installation by others. When someone clicks into this application, a link at the bottom of the page takes him or her to the Dogster & Catster Facebook application page. This is an ideal viral marketing setup. It has information that many people care about, and they make it very easy to spread virally

The new Facebook platform allows developers to create applications within Facebook. So, if you have news or information that might be of interest to people with accounts at Facebook, you may want to consider this. You can go to Mashable Social Networking News to see examples of what others have done.

Debt Predictor Tool

The next site I received an email about was from freelance Web developer Steve Neale. He created a debt predictor tool that gives people an idea of how their finances might look in different financial scenarios. I liked this particular tool because it could potentially prevent what happened to many people who were caught off guard with variable rate mortgages. The need for this kind of tool is particularly timely. Steve saw a common need in the financial marketplace and was able to quickly create a tool to help meet that need.

I might suggest that Steve use a "Send to a Friend" button and other means to help this tool go viral. Once you create something that deserves true link love, you want your visitors to have every opportunity to spread your content virally. This might include links to social bookmarking sites or social news sites.

Be a Purple Cow

Lastly, I would like to tell you about keynote speaker Seth Godin's message at a Search Engine Strategies conference in Toronto, Canada. As you know, Godin is a highly renowned marketing guru.

His premise is that there is simply too much clutter in today's marketing world. As marketers, we deal with all the noise by making more noise. Ultimately, we rarely say anything much different from our competitors. Godin believes the way to differentiate yourself is by being remarkable. You must create something people want to talk about. To do this, you must love your product. You must tell the story that makes it remarkable. And instead of trying to sell to people who don't know you, sell to people who are already listening. From there, allow these people to spread your story. "The idea that spreads, wins!" His advice works for traditional marketers as well as Web marketers.

Godin uses his field of cows story to

illustrate this. A field of cows is nothing to talk about. They're all the same, and they're all doing the same thing. As you drive past a field of cows, surely no one in your car is going to notice them. However, if one of those cows happens to be purple, everyone in your car would certainly talk about it. In fact, you might even stop the car and take a picture. You might upload it to Facebook and tell them you saw a purple cow. A purple cow is worth talking about. If you want to win the link love game, you need to be a purple cow.

A Tale of Two Links

I recently had the opportunity to get two great links. The outcomes were very different. I got one and I lost one. This is the story of how that all transpired and how you can benefit from my success and failure.

First the good news. I got a link from CNET! I was totally psyched about it.

I wish I could say I achieved this link through my awesome, masterful powers of link prowess. However, I got the link due to sheer luck. I was in the right place at the right time.

I was standing around my trade show booth at SES San Jose, minding my own business. You know: chatting up the passersby, staring too long at the pretty booth models. Certain that the last lead was my ticket to massive fortunes.

Then it happened.

A CNET editor quickly came to my booth

asking what I knew about the black hat vs. white hat SEO debate. He was putting together a story about what is and isn't acceptable from a search engine standpoint.

But he was running late and wasn't really sure he could talk to me. I knew this was my chance for a touch of notoriety. So I wanted to give him something interesting. I wanted to give him something quick. I wanted to give him something print-worthy.

There's a quote I often recall: The harder I work, the luckier I get. That quote is the essence of what happened in this moment.

I've spent years studying the search marketing industry. I've been running a Web marketing company since 1999. I've spent years writing about this industry in white papers, blogs, Web sites, and a variety of discussion forums. And I've spent years honing my presentation capabilities.

I've been a member of Toastmasters to help

develop my public speaking skills. I publish a slew of videos primarily on Web marketing but also on a variety of other topics that interest me. And I take virtually every speaking engagement offered me. This helps keep my name in the general business community. And it helps me stay sharp in giving presentations.

After all those years of work understanding our industry and being able to communicate in interesting, effective ways, I was able to be ready for two minutes of an interview that resulted in some really prime recognition.

Years of work for two minutes.

That's often how life works. The harder I work, the luckier I get. I work and work and work, and then I get a break. A small window opens for a brief moment and I get a chance to slip through.

Getting links from reporters and editors is usually like this. You have to train endlessly so you're ready for the window.

So, the actual getting of this link was total, complete luck. I was just in the right place at the right time. I'd be overstating my position if I said it was anything different. I was just some random guy this editor happened across.

But I had been studying for that meeting for the last decade.

Be ready. Links come to you in many ways.

Now for the bad news. Not long after this article got posted I got a voicemail from a major law publication. The person on the voicemail wanted to get my opinion with what was happening with FindLaw and Google. FindLaw was having some disputes with Google about allegedly selling links. This editor wanted my opinion on this situation.

I got the voicemail not long after she left it. But when I heard it, it was late in the day. I was tired. I decided to call her the next day.

As things happen, there were things going on in the morning at the office. I didn't get a chance to call her until mid-afternoon. I thought this was OK because she was on the West Coast and would just be starting her day.

When I called, she answered her phone straight away. She was extremely nice as she told me she had all the information she needed for her article.

I missed my window. I waited too long and didn't give her the proper attention.

Deadlines wait for no person. No preparation in the world will give you a grace period for taking your sweet time getting back to a busy editor.

The moral of this story: be ready. A great link can come to you at a moment's notice. If you don't pounce on it, you very likely will see it slip through your fingers.

Santa Claus

Santa's Claus, a savvy Web marketer? I thought it would be interesting to look at three main Santa Claus websites: northpole.com, santaclaus.com, and claus.com.

Wouldn't the real Santa Claus want Claus.com to be number one? Or wouldn't he prefer the logical domain choice, SantaClaus.com? Yet look at these Open Site Explorer stats:

	Northpole.com	SantaClaus.com	claus.com
Page Authority:	58	44	48
Page MozRank:	5.47	3.5	3.84
Page MozTrust:	5.65	5.07	5.34
Internal Followed Links:	3,244	16	0
External Followed Links:	323	21	24
Total Internal Links:	3,447	16	0
Total External Links:	359	33	31
Total Links:	3,806	49	31
Followed Linking Root Domains:	120	13	18
Total Linking Root Domains:	136	22	21
Linking C Blocks:	100	20	20

Northpole.com beats the other two across the board.

Link Building: Check Indexed Content

The answer comes down to what each site has to offer. It's easy to get a quick picture of which site is better simply by looking at which site has the most content indexed. Look at these numbers:

Claus.com: 831 pages.

Santaclaus.com: 2,290 pages.

Northpole.com: 10,200 pages.

Without even going to the sites, you can tell northpole.com has been working harder on content than the other sites have.

Link Building: Does Content Resonate?

Visiting northpole.com doesn't disappoint, either. There are tons of things for visitors to do.

Check out the Elves' Game Chest. There's Disco Dancing Santa, where you can change the scenery, Santa's dance moves, and the accompanying songs. Santa even has a cookbook.

No Santa site would be complete without a mailroom where you can write to Santa. There are a bunch of interactive things that make writing Santa extra special fun.

Link Building: Fulfill Your Mission

The people at northpole.com sincerely want to be the best Santa Claus site online. Honestly, I don't know why they go to all the effort. They ask for donations to help with expenses.

The "Toy Shop" page sends you to some educational toys at Amazon where northpole.com is an affiliate. That's definitely not a get rich quick scheme. They don't even have Google AdSense ads on the site.

Their mission statement hasn't changed since 1996: providing visitors an enriched Christmas experience through a totally child-safe, innovative, imaginative, and yet traditional holiday Web site.

Link Building: Transparency and Sincerity

In the social media world, we're finding nonprofits adapt quicker than their corporate counterparts. Nonprofits are spending more time in places like Facebook, Twitter and YouTube. The reason is easy to deduce. Nonprofit organizations, for the most part, care more about what they're doing than profit-based organizations.

It's easier to reach out to the online community to tell a sincere, compassionate story. This is more difficult in the traditional business world because who loves their screws, batteries, and financial services?

Who has enough love for their company to create something as well done as northpole.com? Maybe the owner? Maybe.

The online world has already transformed

business in many ways: globalization of services, flattening of organizations, customer participation in messaging, constant information availability, constant communication. But there's one more change on the horizon.

Link Building: The Secret Truth

One link building topic doesn't get discussed. The companies that will succeed in an online marketplace will have to find love.

They'll have to find appreciation, compassion, understanding, just plain old love, if they want to participate in the global conversation everyone's having about goods and services. The companies that continue to yell and stomp their marketing feet until people buy something are not long for the 21st century business world.

So, if you can't find an ounce of love for the batteries you sell, what about your company can you love? Is it your community contributions? Is it the ecological sustainability you are promoting for your company and your community? Is it the dedication you have to your team?

If you want links, you have to find something you truly love, tap into the humanity of your business, and build it on your site. You simply can't build something that's link-worthy any other way.

Why would people work so hard to create the best Santa Claus Web site year after year and make little to no money? The only answer can be love. They love Christmas and they love Santa.

Obama's Link Strategy Fuels Election Victory

Without a doubt, Barack Obama creamed John McCain in 2008 when it came to links. At the time, Yahoo Site Explorer showed nearly 2 million links to www.barackobama.com, but just over 900,000 links to www.johnmccain.com.

Let's look closer at these numbers so you can learn from them and possibly apply them to your own situation.

Look at the Landscape

According to data released by Rubicon Consulting, "Democrats are more active online than Republicans. Democrats are more likely to participate in online communities, and say they're more heavily influenced in their voting decisions by information they find online."

It's easy to see that the Internet is more

friendly to liberals and Democrats just by perusing the leading headlines at Digg. During that election these were some of the top headlines in the world and business section:

898 diggs: Cavuto to McCain: You have no economic convictions

1,528 diggs: The Republican Party is dead

2,021 diggs: If Obama wins Virginia - it's over

For reasons I don't want to speculate on, liberal-leaning people favor the Internet, so McCain had an uphill battle to begin with. Obama's base was more saturated in the overall landscape.

Consider the Liberal Audience

If you have a product or service that caters to issues that Democrats care about, you'll probably have an easier time gathering interest and links than a business that serves a Republican audience.

To take this understanding a step further, apply it to other audiences. For example, more people search online for cars and houses than excavator parts. So, you would probably have an easier time garnering links to a site that offered interesting information or entertainment about cars and houses compared to excavators.

That's not to say you can't get links for an excavator parts Web site or a conservative issues Web site. They just might be harder to come by.

While conservatives seem to be getting somewhat better at this, they still remain behind.

As of my typing of this sentence, Rush Limbaugh has Tweeted 42 times, has followed 0 people and has 220k followers.

This is in comparison to Rachel Maddow with 2235 tweets. She follows 1354 and has 2.5 million followers. Also, remember that Obama's Web site was built for interaction and community since the beginning. I reported back in August 2007 how Obama was leading the social media revolution by having a larger Internet presence and a more energized base.

One of the most visionary, forward-thinking actions of Obama's campaign was hiring Chris Hughes, the co-founder of Facebook, to act as coordinator of online organizing within the Obama presidential campaign on My.BarackObama.com, the campaign's online social networking Web site.

Ultimately, they built a link strategy right into the core of their online strategy. Granted, they wouldn't have classified it as a link building campaign -- it was a social networking campaign. However, links are a direct product of a successful Web site.

They didn't say, "Now that we have a Web site, why don't we give people a place to participate?" Instead, they said, "How can we make a Web site that continually energizes our supporters and becomes a major resource online?"

How the Walmart Grinch Stole Black Friday Link Love

The blog post, "Walmart Sends DMCA Notice to SearchAllDeals, TechCrunch" on Search Engine Watch's Blog was extremely interesting on several levels.

DMCA is the Digital Millennium Copyright Act. Wal-Mart told SearchAllDeals and TechCrunch to immediately take down links to Black Friday deals that weren't supposed to be out before November 24. SearchAllDeals and TechCrunch didn't publish the content. They just linked to it.

One provision, called Section 512, of the DMCA generally says companies are off the hook if they remove copyrighted content promptly when it's brought to their attention.

Napster shouted "512" back in the day, but it didn't work for them. The 512 "safe harbor" is there to typically let hosting companies off the hook for legal liability, as long as they don't ignore copyright infringement and if they remove the stuff when notified.

In the Black Friday Wal-Mart situation, they're all in a tizzy about "linking to infringing content."

The gist of it all is that, in the U.S., it appears that it could be illegal to link to infringing content. And you could be in for some serious legal trouble if you don't take down the link. So, if SearchAllDeals and TechCrunch got in trouble for linking to these Black Friday deals; your business could find itself in the soup too with errant links.

So... I have three thoughts on all this:

1: Be careful linking to stuff that is potentially infringing on copyright. You could actually find yourself in some legal hot water. As they point out over at WebTVwire.com, if it's illegal to link to copyright material, does that mean it's illegal to write an infringing Web address on a piece of paper and give it to a friend? Who knows? Just beware and be careful.

2: Are you serious, Wal-Mart? Here's some free advice you might be able to understand, Wal-Mart: Links good.

3: Maybe Wal-Mart is the most genius retail company in the world. I mean, the only Black Friday ad I *had* to get my hands on early was the Wal-Mart ad. And it was the same boring ad as always. But the whole scene became much more interesting with this added twist of irate legal saber rattling.

Link Philosophy: Know Thyself, but Care about More

Love or hate it; I'm a passionate guy. I know this about myself and I embrace it. My personal opinions and "philosophies" about topics like Link Building within Web Marketing are part of my own Link Bait. My passionate personal ideas make me stand out in a sea of marketing experts. Standing out, however, is tricky. You open yourself to criticism. You accidentally leave holes in your arguments for all to see and you might actually misrepresent facts.

But here's dirty little secret number one about standing out and link love. None of the details matter. In fact, sometimes leaving gaps for people to attack you can be a good thing. Here's an example.

A blogger and SEO critic, Jeremy Schoemaker, took offense to one of my videos.

He has this shtick he does where he talks about how SEOs suck and then his followers pretty much line up in agreement with whatever he says.

The thing is, he uses basic SEO principles all the time. Case in point is this article. He comes up for my company name, my personal name, and the phrase "Akron SEO." It's because the title of the article is: "Akron SEO Sage Lewis of SageRock WTF?"

He optimized the hell out of it.

That article caused me a lot of stress. I was shocked by it. There were hundreds of comments. Everybody was out to get me. The people-pleaser in me still doesn't like thinking about it in-depth.

But here's the thing... that was probably the best thing that ever happened to me online.

I received a lot of private support by people who saw it. They didn't all come out on his blog. Maybe they were afraid they'd get a similar thrashing. So, that was nice.

I feel it elevated my status. Getting put up on Shoemoney's blog is major exposure. Also, I didn't feel like I did anything wrong. He had a point of view and I had a point of view. He just tried his hardest to make me look incompetent and stupid.

Lean forward here. I'm about to tell you dirty little secret number two about standing out. Part of an effective PR response to these kinds of things is to keep the controversy going.

When you get hit with one of these flare-ups, it's a gift to not be wasted. You *want* to issue a response, not so that the pain of it recedes, but so it all stays in the news. The finesse comes in as you turn the story back to you, but in a more favorable light. You're the good person. You run an honorable business. You only want to do what is best for your customers.

Think about it like the comedy it is. You start on a high note. Everything is humming along fine. Then the controversy happens, which is the low dip. And finally, the hero prevails, pushing you out of the trough and back into the light.

Your customers and potential clients want the resolution. They want a response. Not giving them one ruins the whole plot. While these kinds of things are stressful and painful, realize that they're also rare treasures. So go forth and don't be afraid to mix it up a little. It will keep things interesting, and you almost always come out better for it on the other side. You can file this under both "Promotions" and "Link Building."

Care about More

Great people who are also newsworthy do not typically desire glory. Their greatness comes from dedicating their lives to something bigger than themselves.

Consider Nancy Brinker. After her sister

died from breast cancer at age 36, Brinker felt the outcome might have been better if patients knew more about cancer and its treatment. She went on to start a foundation in her sister's name, The Susan G. Komen Breast Cancer Foundation.

Consider Randy Pausch. After learning his pancreatic cancer was terminal, he conceived of "The Last Lecture." It is an optimistic, upbeat speech on achieving childhood dreams.

What in your life is trial when it could be triumph? What do you care about beyond yourself and your business? Don't be afraid to share it. Not just for link love (which is why you're reading, of course), but also for support, community and to help others who can relate.

Here are some examples of things that get online community support and link love.

Job layoffs: Laying people off is terrible. But what if you cared about where they went after you laid them off? What if you offered a workshop to help them with their resumes, held a networking event with other businesses in your area to help them find a new job or offered training to help them move into a new position? Then your business could create a written process for other companies looking to do the same and put it on your Web site for download.

Helping or Supporting People and Causes:
Reaching out to people starting businesses, or starting anything, is worthy of link love. Help can come in the form of cash, but people also need volunteers, non-profits need discount work, schools need things donated to fundraisers.

SageRock, as an example, regularly hosted events at our former office for a local LGBT group, Plexus. But we forgot to TELL people about it. Well, to be honest, I didn't promote it because I didn't want to come across as a person who does good things just for the marketing value. Get over that. Telling people about how you help isn't just self promotion, it could help others do more in the community. You're a role model.

Personal Failure (AKA: vulnerability): Write about your failures. What are the biggest mistakes you have made? How can you help others avoid the pitfalls that afflicted you? Or what about a dream that you set out to achieve and didn't accomplish? This may sound too personal to you. Maybe you don't want to air your dirty laundry on the Web for everyone to see and judge.

But vulnerability is an essential part of all our commonality as humans. People will be attracted to you because you're sharing a fragile part of you that helps them relate. Additionally, you're helping people who are experiencing similar suffering.

I am also highly influenced by an article

written by Brian Eisenburg: ***What Makes People Buy? 20 Reasons Why.***
http://www.bryaneisenberg.com/what-makes-people-buy-20-reasons-why/

He lists and explains the "forces that influence whether people buy." They are:

➢ Basic Needs

➢ Convenience

➢ Replacement

➢ Scarcity

➢ Emotional Vacuum

➢ Lower prices

➢ Great Value

➢ Name Recognition

➢ Fad or Innovation

➢ Compulsory Purchase

➢ Ego Stroking

➢ Niche Identity

➢ Peer Pressure

➢ The "Girl Scout Cookie Effect"

➢ Reciprocity or Guilt

- ➤ Empathy
- ➤ Addiction
- ➤ Fear
- ➤ Indulgence

I love this article because it gets to the heart of what motivates people psychologically. In link building you are, after all, trying to sell people on the concept of linking to you. If they buy, then you get the link. You'll have an easier time in the whole process if you understand people's basic motivations.

Conclusion

Why do we want more links? Why should someone link to us? Why does anyone care about our site? These are the questions that must be answered if one wishes to drive the link economy.

The underlying reason for all of this is that if enough people link to me, I'll rise in the search engine rankings. Once I rise in the rankings, more people will come to my site. With more people coming to my site, it's more likely they'll buy what I'm selling. The more I sell, the richer I become. The richer I become, the more sites I can find on the search engines so I can buy more stuff.

Do you see the whirling little circle that keeps spinning and spinning for no reason other than to buy and sell stuff?

There's an unspoken undercurrent that this

Sisyphean gerbil wheel has happiness at the end of it, much like the pot of gold at the end of a rainbow. I'm not convinced the quality of life for the original Americans who lived here has proportionately increased with the wealth the U.S. has amassed to date.

You may say, "Thank you for your philosophical pontification of the American condition, Sage. But I am reading this book to learn how to get more links."

Yes, but I believe understanding the capitalist condition is the key to getting links.

You see, every time you ask for a link, the same thought process goes on in the head of the person who's considering giving you a link. "This person wants my link so he can get rich." But the anonymous person at the other end of the link request doesn't care one bit about you getting rich. He has his own self-centered, egotistical ambitions to worry about.

If you want links -- genuine, high quality,

community building, link love – you've got to step off the gerbil wheel. It is a necessity so that you can muster up enough energy to do something creative that *deserves* links.

I'm sorry if you wanted tips and tricks. In the end, it's just not that easy. Create a cause. Find a passion. Entertain. Engage. Make a difference online. Only then can you reach out and build real links.

About Sage

Sage lives with his wife Rocky and son, Indiana in Akron Ohio. They have a big time of it all camping, swimming in their above-ground pool and hot tub. It's a charmed and charming life.

Sage is nothing if not passionate. He loves everything he does. He sees the digital landscape as the greatest communication evolution in the history of humanity.

He has been the Professional In Residence at The University of Findlay. He regularly teaches SEO, social media, HTML and other courses at Cleveland State University.

He speaks to organizations, companies and associations coast to coast on the strategic uses of SEO and social media.

Sage is the founder and president of SageRock.com - a digital marketing agency helping businesses of all sizes become more successful online since 1999.

You can find Sage online at these places:

https://twitter.com/sagerock
https://www.facebook.com/sagerock
http://www.youtube.com/sagerock
sage@sagerock.com

www.ingramcontent.com/pod-product-compliance
Lightning Source LLC
Chambersburg PA
CBHW060015210326
41520CB00009B/897